From … Train to Ph.D.

A Journey of Survival,

Gambling Addiction,

Homelessness, Redemption

& Self-Improvement

By Dr. Michael P. Williams

Foreword by

Earl "the Pearl" Monroe

A Journey of Survival, Gambling Addiction, Homelessness, Redemption & Self-Improvement

By

Dr. Michael P. Williams

Foreword

By Earl "The Pearl" Monroe

ISBN; 978-0-578-83694-2

Published by Outerbridge Books, LLC

Cover & Interior Design: George Rodrigues

To Order additional copies of this book;

Website: http://www.outerbridgebooks.com

Email: hello@drmichaelpwilliams.com

Dedication

To My Mother Ruth

& My Mother Mary

Thank you for watching over me

FOREWORD BY EARL "THE PEARL" MONROE

I met Dr. Michael P Williams at a fundraiser for a new basketball league that he was starting. It was well attended by his associates and celebrities. Some of the people in attendance I knew, and there were a few pro basketball players that played for the New York Knicks. For me at that time, it was just a cocktail reception and I had no real relationship with Michael, except just being there and enjoying the festivities. As time went on, we got to know each other better, mainly because we enjoyed some of the same things and shared opinions, and spoke freely about life and what life had to offer. At the time he was the owner of an employment staffing agency and enjoyed playing basketball. He was an affable and outgoing person and thought owning a non-profit basketball league would bridge together with a few things he cared about…business, basketball, and people. A New Yorker, who grew up in the South Bronx, he certainly was in the right city to fulfill his dreams.

As we got to know each other better Michael talked about his family and how life was being brought up in the South Bronx. He told of his eleven siblings and the foster home he was in and how he went from being a homeless man with an addiction to gambling to becoming the CEO of his own staffing company. It's an amazing story. He spoke about the ups and downs of life and how he dealt with it, and his chance meeting with a person in the subway that changed his life and his destiny. As he spoke, his story became more and more fascinating.

In his book "From The A Train to Ph.D.; A Journey of Survival, Gambling Addiction, Homelessness, Redemption & Self-Improvement", Dr. Williams talked about all aspects of his life. You could say, "He let it all hang out" A book must do more than just chronologically report the actions of life. It must be authentic and inventive in the way it touches lives. It has to be informative and give resolve. It's not about the struggles, but the redemptive nature of overcoming those struggles and how you use that to develop the person you have become. I recommend reading this book because the pouring of emotions of this book causes you to examine and re-examine your own life and help your define your own identity. That's what this book is about. It's both exhilarating and sad at the same time. It's not your typical rags to riches story, but a story of the real challenges and triumphs in the life of Dr. Michael P. Williams

A NOTE FROM OTHERS

You will not find another life story quite like Dr. Michael Williams. His journey was extraordinary and illuminating. Simply remarkable. This memoir is harrowing, witty, and unforgettable. A reminder that despite the challenges we face today, we must never surrender. His story is all about the pursuit of a dream.

- Dick Barnett, Ph.D. New York Knicks' Legend, NBA Hall of Fame, and Author "Without Rhyme or Reason"

Mike Williams shows us in his gripping story what life on the streets looks like, especially, for troubled foster kids, and the problem gambler. The book is inspirational. For some people, this book could provide insight for a better way of life

- Josh Kosman, New York Post, Writer, and Author "The Buyout of America"

As I read his book, I could not put it down. It's a real-life story. Gut-wrenching, astonishing, and powerful. His life is also a triumph. He writes about his struggles, gambling addiction, and his recovery. Even with my many years of experience, I was spellbound. We all face some challenges today, Yet, Mike is living reassurance that the human spirit is indomitable. A must-read.

- Arnie Wexler, Council Compulsive Gambling of NJ, and Author "All Bets Are Off"

We met three decades ago in the same recovery group that I attend today. His story is amazing, and inspirational. Mike proves to be a powerful example of faith and determination. The book is electrifying and he takes you on his journey once again. Yet, there is light at the end of the tunnel. His mission today is to carry the message of hope. I plan to give this book to a lot of people that I know, some are facing real challenges, particularly, the people who are facing long-term unemployment.

- David Schlamm CEO & President, City Connections Realty, Inc. New York City

Michael's story will inspire and encourage you! When you read about the obstacles he has surmounted to achieve academic and business success, you'll want to pass on his story to friends who are struggling. His life story has motivated me to want to accomplish more.

- Glen Kleinknecht, CRU INNER CITY, Director of Expansion

ABOUT THE AUTHOR

Michael Williams is a native New Yorker from the South Bronx. He grew up one of twelve children who lived in a single-parent home with his mother Ruth Williams. Ruth died on March 26, 1970, and the family was separated. Most of William's siblings were taken into foster care. Williams spent five years at the Richmond Hill Group Home for boys in South Ozone Park Queens. Because of the conflicts with residents and abuse by staff experienced in the group home life, he took to the streets to search for his family. He spent several years as a homeless man living in the New York City subway system. He also developed a gambling addiction. A chance meeting with a person in the subway changed the direction of Williams' life and his destiny. He first found work as a security guard and then as a sales representative for an employment agency. By 1991, Williams had become President and CEO of United Personnel Agency, Inc. In 2004, he founded the Worldwide Basketball Association (WBA), along with NBA legend Dr. Dick Barnett, and with help from Earl "the Pearl" Monroe. The WBA nonprofit organization provided sports programs for adults and motivational workshops for youth. In 2011, Williams enrolled in a doctoral program and began working on his dissertation. He is currently a Professor in the Public Management Department at John Jay College of Criminal Justice. Michael now has over thirty-seven years of abstinence from gambling and continues to work with individuals and groups in recovery. His goal today is to carry the message of hope and encouragement to people everywhere, to disadvantaged individuals, to the long-term unemployed, to people facing addiction, and to young men of color.

Author's Note

This book is a work of nonfiction. I have written the events truthfully as I have recalled them. I have changed some names of individuals to respect their privacy. The events depicted come from my own recollection, and are not meant to represent any precise period or event. The events are told in a way of what happened to me in keeping with the true meaning of the experiences as they have impacted my life. Any information provided herein offers no guarantee of success to any one person. I have rendered the events faithfully as I have recalled them.

From The A Train To PhD

INTRODUCTION

In early March of 2020, we began to hear reports that COVID-19 had infected over 19,000 people in the United States, and some 247 had died from the virus. It seemed like the virus had hit New York overnight. We had no idea that the virus would rage over the months ahead, and cause mass destruction and death. Even at the start, it was difficult not to feel the stress and anxiety that was invading every home. I worked for a company that was struggling as a result of the pandemic. So I was making plans to start a new business. I designed a business model for a new publishing company and a new staffing agency. I decided to explore all options. I could sense that trouble was on the horizon. I arranged a meeting with a group of investors. I decided to move as fast as I could.

My instincts were accurate. By the end of April, the staffing firm where I had worked for 16 years called me to terminate my position. I was terminated on a conference call. No severance pay, just good-bye. It was a hard blow, but I did not panic. I was still working as a college professor at John Jay College of Criminal Justice. However, the loss of my position as Vice President of the staffing firm represented a huge loss, nearly 75 percent of my income was gone. Also, I could not apply for unemployment insurance while I was teaching. So, I decided to focus all of my attention on the meetings with the investment group and to get the new company up and running as quickly as possible.

However, I was surprised to learn that I would need to travel to a real estate office in Queens, New York for the meeting with the investors. The guidelines about wearing a mask and social distancing were still developing. So I agreed to meet in person with that group of investors. The meeting would take place in a large room, with just the four of us. Oddly, that meeting was scheduled to take place near my old neighborhood in South Ozone Park, Queens. I had moved away from the neighborhood in 1976, and I had mixed feelings about going back to that part of town. There were a lot of bad memories.

A lot has changed since 1976. I have been an entrepreneur for many years and had operated my staffing agency and a non-profit organization. I have been in the employment staffing business for nearly three decades, and I have been a professor at John Jay College of Criminal Justice for about four years.

Some of the past years were good and some bad. But my overall journey was very rough and I choose not to look back. Now, I found myself preparing for a meeting with this new investment group, and I was back in my old neighborhood. As I arrived in South Ozone Park, I started having some flashbacks.

I had been raised one of twelve children in a single-parent home in the South Bronx. While money was very tight for my mother, she filled the home with love. That all changed on a cold March morning when my mother Ruth Hearns Williams died suddenly. She had just turned forty years of age. Of the three stepfathers that I could remember, no one ever stayed with us for more than a year.

The day after Mother died, our home was like a scene out of the movie *The Body Snatchers*. There were social workers everywhere. My younger brothers and I were in shock as we were ushered out of the house. We were all very quiet. We were in a state of denial. We were leaving our home, but we were sure we would be living together again. We were wrong.

My younger sisters, however, seemed to know that our family was being ripped apart. They both began to weep. The social workers tried to keep them calm. Then the van arrived.

Some of my siblings were placed in foster care, a few were put into group homes, and some were put up for adoption. Because of my age, I was selected to go to the Richmond Hill Group Home, in South Ozone Park, a home for boys who had lost one or both parents and were, therefore, wards of the state. Once I arrived, I felt out of place and was filled with fear and anxiety. One day I was living in the South Bronx with my mother and family, and the next I was in a strange house living with ten boys I had never met before.

All I wanted was to know when I would see my brothers and sisters. I feared I would never see them again. I did not understand how a twelve-year-old could lose his entire family and not even get an answer from the so-called people in charge.

So my story is about a journey to reunite a family. It is a story about survival and redemption. It is also a story about addiction. When you lose your family, and you feel responsible for your younger siblings-you are conflicted. That can be very painful for a young boy. You may decide to search for a painkiller, as I did.

In my case, my painkiller was gambling, mostly at dice games and later on at the racetracks. I loved the action. That feeling of being on a winning streak was like no feeling in the world. I sometimes had pockets full of money, and I could not spend the money fast enough or handle the excitement.

Unfortunately, my gambling addiction only led to many years of depression, anger, inadequacy, and self-destruction. On several occasions, I nearly lost my life. For many people, compulsive gambling remains one of the most baffling of all addictions.

The greatest thing for the gambler is betting and winning, and the second greatest thing is betting and losing. When I finally hit rock bottom, I was consistently consumed by despair, stress, shame, resentment and anxiety.

I was soon homeless and sleeping in an abandoned building in Brooklyn. Soon I was sleeping in the subway. One night in an abandoned building, I played a very dangerous game with a loaded gun. I had nothing else to lose. That memory remains the most repugnant and cowardly moment I have ever experienced.

It is truly a miracle that I'm here today to tell my story. Part of that miracle are the interventions that took place in my life. They were each unique, and each made all the difference in my life. Those interventions involved people from every walks of life, both white and black people, people of every color in the rainbow. So if I ever became a racist, I would also be a hypocrite.

One of the interventions consisted of a twenty-minute meeting with a stranger who brought me a cup of coffee in the subway while I was still homeless. It was not so much what he said as what he did that changed my life. So, this book is also about the power of intervention.

After the last intervention, my life moved in a different direction. One of my main reasons for writing this book is to document my experiences and try to carry a message of hope to the next person. This is how it happened for me many years ago, and I hope to never forget.

Today I cannot explain how I survived those lean years living on the streets. I do not know how I managed the deep depression that consumed my life and my soul for many years. I find it difficult to believe that I was fortunate to eventually get on my feet, first by working for as a security guard, next a staffing firm and then start my employment agency. I went on to provide jobs for thousands of people. I was also blessed to have the opportunity to return to school. I've completed both my master's degree and my Ph.D. I now teach at one of the best institutions, John Jay College of Criminal Justice. Ironically, I was chasing "the dream world" as a gambler for years, and yet, I became a winner by not making a bet.

Yes, I was born poor and black, and part of a large family living in the ghetto of the South Bronx. I've told that story many times to anyone who would listen. However, it was Shakespeare who once said, "To thine own self be true." The real reason I had been homeless and living a destitute life for so long was not so much about being black or poor but was about the fact that I was a gambling junkie. Until I faced that fact, my life could not change for the better. I needed to be true to myself. I needed to face the enemy within.

I now want to carry a message of hope to people who needs to confront addiction, to the person who has experienced long-term unemployment, to any person who has faced depression, struggled with self-sabotage, to the person who experienced or is dealing with homelessness, to the person who is considering returning to school, or the person who struggled with low self-esteem. In particular, I hope to reach young, unemployed black men who still want to believe that it is important to "have a dream."

So on that day in late April, I arrived at the real estate office for my meeting in South Ozone Park Queens. I waited for my meeting to start with this new group of investors, I sat across the street from the Richmond Hill Group Home for Boys and reminisced about my experiences when I lived there. I remembered my journey to find my family. I re-lived some of the highs and lows of my journey. I remembered the pain and abuse. I remembered my determination to keep the faith. I remembered some wise words I was once told. I believe that we must remember the mistakes of the past, or we are doomed to repeat those mistakes.

PART ONE

CHAPTER 1

"If I am not for myself, who will be for me? But if I am only for myself, who am I? If not now, when?"

Hillel the Elder

ALL ABOUT FAMILY

My mother made a bet and lost. She did not have the money to pay up. So, she made a compromise. As it happened, my mother was passing by a local bar called the Blue Diamond Lounge located in the Morrisania section of the Bronx. My mother, eight months pregnant with me, stopped to talk with the bar owner. She told him that she had a hunch.

She said, “I know for sure I’m going to have a girl this time. I can feel it! I’ve had three sons in a row. This one is a girl.”

The bartender replied, “I think you’re having a boy, that’s what I think.”

My mother saw an opening. “I’ll bet you five dollars that I’m having a girl!”

“It’s a bet!”

In 1958, five dollars was a lot of money for my mother, but she was so confident that I would be a girl that she made the wager. I arrived three days later on February 21, 1958, at a quarter past seven in the morning. When my mother arrived home from the hospital with me, she saw the bar owner and confessed that she did not have the five dollars to pay off the debt.

“Don’t worry about the money,” the bar owner replied. “But do me a favor. Name your son after me since I never had any kids.” My mother replied “Ok, Mike”

So, I got my name because of a lost bet. The conditions we lived under were hard. Often we did not have food in the house. But, there was a lot of love in our home. We lived in a small tenement apartment at 480 St. Paul’s Place in the Bronx. The apartment was on the sixth floor, it felt like a long climb. At that time, it was just Richard, Gary, and Frank in the home. Then me. My other older siblings Harold and Barbara were living with their father, Lester Lewis. We only lived at St. Paul’s Place for a few years but I still remember the old, dark brick church across the street. I still remember the sounds of a barking dog late at night and the sounds of police sirens. I saw a car chase, it was like watching cops and robbers in real-time.

I remember one story my mother shared with me from that time, something that happened a few months after she brought me home from the hospital. She was in the kitchen preparing dinner. Suddenly, she heard a loud splashing sound, and then she heard me crying in my crib. She immediately dropped pots and dishes and ran towards the bedroom. When she entered, the entire room was illuminated. She saw three men standing over my crib. She said it looked like they were praying over me. She panicked and tried to reach for me and grab me from the crib. However, she found that she was paralyzed. The three men continued praying for a few minutes. Then, as quickly as it had started, the room went dark again. Suddenly, the three men disappeared.

Now, my mother could move again, and she noticed that the room was soaked with water. Water was everywhere! The walls were soaked. The floor was soaked. I was soaked in my crib. She told me that it took her hours to mop up all the water. Eventually, the room was back to normal, but she never forgot that event and she was convinced that I was a blessed child. Over years, I would think about the "three angels" who prayed at my bedside. Especially during the darkest days, including when I almost lost my life, I would wonder if the angels were looking over me.

Then we moved into another tenement building at 415 East 145th Street just off Willis Avenue in the South Bronx. Even though our new apartment consisted of two units combined into one, it felt even smaller than our last place because now there were more children, twelve of us, and different men in and out of my mother's life. Richard and Gary were starting to grow, both looked like college football players. Frank was tall and thin. The younger kids were surprisingly quiet, and we spent most of our time watching the television. There were my sisters Susan, and Ruth. and my younger brothers Nat, Juan, Gerald, and Gregory.

The building was a six-story walk-up and we lived on the fifth floor. The rooms—four bedrooms, two bathrooms, a living room, and the kitchen—were very small. In the kitchen were a small table, a radio, and a few simple pictures of flowers on the wall. The kitchen table was mainly for preparing meals, and sometimes my mother would host a weekend card game with some of our neighbors. During dinner, we sat in the living room and ate our food in front of the television. There were only four stations on the TV, so every night we watched game shows like Password and serials like Batman and Robin and Superman. My mother had a lot of religious statues in her room and would burn incense every night, to keep evil spirits away. She loved chocolate candy bars and butter pecan ice cream. Even now, I only eat butter pecan ice cream. If she could afford to buy her favorite incense, it had a raspberry favor. Most nights she used the incense that smells like burned rubber. She would burn sugar to make incense. It was really bad. I still suffer from a sinus condition today, some five decades later.

Our building was like a little United Nations. Black families, white families, Puerto Rican families, and other families, all shared the same small apartment building. It was odd. We were somewhat aware of racism, but not much. It was different living in the South Bronx because most of the time you did not care if your neighbor was white or not. We all needed food. So that was not the problem. Now some people were jealous of others, and that was a problem. Yet, for the most part, we were all in this hell together. For instance, an older Jewish lady named Mabel Rosenbaum lived downstairs, and we all noticed the numbers she had tattooed on her arm. She had been in a concentration camp in Poland during World War II. Somehow, she survived and found her way to America, to the South Bronx, to a predominantly black neighborhood (though I am sure the neighborhood was probably all white when she first moved into it). Mabel was in her mid-70s. My mother realized that Mabel could no longer take care of herself, could no longer feed, or even clean herself, so my mother moved her into our fourth bedroom and I was moved onto the couch. My mother had a good heart. However, moving Mabel into the house was also about economics. My mother could now take care of Mabel and she could also control Mabel's monthly check.

This kind of "thinking out of the box" was how people learned to survive in the ghetto of the South Bronx. The residents of our building fought for their lives, confronting severe poverty and depression every day, and the common goal was to have a meal at least once a day. Most people cannot understand life in the ghetto, but we used what I call the "economies of scale." Every person in the building was aware of their neighbors' inventory. My mother knew which neighbor had a good supply of rice, which neighbor had sugar, and which neighbor had vegetables. The neighbors likewise knew that my mother often had a good supply of flour and salt. My mother would send me to a neighbor carrying two cups of rice, and I would come back with two cups of flour.

It was an extraordinary system, this economy of scale, and yet I've never heard anyone talk about it. I have not even read about it in books. This system of "economies of scale" might have been the greatest weapon that these families had in their fight for survival.

However, it became clear to me at a young age that my mother was fighting a losing battle.

For Ruth Williams, a good day was being able to feed her family. It was a real challenge for her to find food, as a single mother on welfare, to feed a family of thirteen people every single day. Often, my mother would make a big pot of stew, enough for all of us, and that made her feel like her day was a big success. This would make her smile. My mother had a mesmerizing smile. She could sometimes charm the local grocery clerk. However, she had to achieve this task seven days a week, and unfortunately, she didn't have that many good days. Her everyday life was consumed by stress, fear, and anxiety. As a result, we missed supper quite a few nights.

One thing that created a great deal of stress for my mother was the threat of witchcraft. Oddly, despite our struggles, we had some neighbors who were jealous of my mother. They did not wish us well. My mother was even convinced that some of our neighbors hated her. They hated the fact that she had a family of twelve and yet managed to survive. They accused her of being a welfare queen and resented the fact she got more money from welfare than they did. Some of the neighbors, my mother believed, hoped that she would just drop dead one day.

I would come home from school and find strange items in front of our apartment door that confirmed her fears. Someone placed the leg of a rooster or some animal bones. Once, as soon as I walked over the threshold, my left leg hurt. I could feel some sharp pain. It was difficult to walk. After a few hours, I could walk again.

However, my mother freaked out. This occurrence confirmed her belief that our neighbors wanted to see our family suffer. She began to fight back in every way she could. She splashed holy water and oils around the apartment. She prayed every day and burned incense every night, the stuff that smelled like burned rubber. She visited a lady who was a gypsy to purchase more candles and ointments. I was convinced that the gypsy lady was a con, but my mother bought it hook, line and sinker. She spent her entire welfare check on candles and statues. I believed we missed many meals because she spent so much money fighting witchcraft.

She finally had to explain racism to us, it became difficult to avoid. I remember sitting next to my mother one night as we were watching Password. Suddenly, the program was interrupted by the words “Special Bulletin” running across the screen. An announcer said, “The Reverend Martin Luther King, Jr., was shot this evening.”

My mother became very quiet and dropped her head down. I looked up at her. I asked, “Mom, do you think he is going to die?”

She replied, “I don't know, Michael. He was a good man, and we knew that something bad like this would happen to him.” Password came back on, and we continued watching the show.

Then, another special bulletin: “Dr. Martin Luther King, Jr., was killed tonight.” I again looked to my mother and asked, “Mommy, only a few minutes ago he was Reverend Martin Luther King Jr. Now, they said Dr. Martin Luther King Jr., was killed. How did he become a doctor that fast?”

My mother paused for a moment and then said very slowly, “Well, he's dead now, Michael. People will be calling him a lot of things.” That moment was gripping, and yet I would not fully understand its meaning for many years to come.

Another big cause of stress for my mother was my oldest brother, Richard. He was often in trouble on the streets and regularly ran away from home. I remember watching my mother late at night as she looked out the window and smoked a cigarette, waiting for Richard to come home while the song “Runaway Child” by The Temptations played on our record player.

All this on top of the concern about where she would get food for her children. Yet, I also saw how hopeful my mother was at times. A man at a racetrack once told me, "If you pray for rain, take an umbrella". So, if you ask for something, be prepared. So strangely, my mom often would believe in these little miracles. Especially, at dinner time.

She might not have any food for dinner one night. Yet, she would put a pot of water on the stove to boil, and she would send me to the grocery store with a note asking the clerk to give us something.

I would return home empty-handed. I would say, "Mom, the man said he can't give you any more food until you pay the bill." Her head would drop for a minute.

Then she would remember another grocery store, and she would write another note. I would take that note to the next grocer. He would also turn me down. I would go home to my mom again and repeat, "The man in the store said he can't give you any more credit until you pay your bill."

She would become desperate, and I could see her fear. But she wouldn't give up. Another note. Another grocery store, further away. And she would fill all our pots with water and put them on the stove to boil.

The pots on the stove were my mother's way of carrying an umbrella. She was getting ready to put food into those pots. So off I went to the next grocery store, this time walking to 149th Street and Third Avenue. This time when I walked into the grocery store, the manager seemed surprised to see me, and he recognized me. He smiled at me, as I handed him the note. Everyone who met my mother remembered her. She was a strikingly beautiful woman, even at the age of thirty-nine. I think that most men that looked at her were quite interested. I watched how they reacted when she walked down the street. However, once they learned she had twelve children, their interest disappeared.

I would take the note she gave me to the local grocery store. I said, "Good afternoon sir, I have a note from my mother." When he read it, his face fell. He shook his head and, again, told me, "I'm sorry, your mother still has an unpaid bill here."

I walked back home empty-handed yet again. When I entered the apartment I felt the heat of the boiling pots of water in the kitchen. My mom looked at me and started to cry. She had exhausted every possibility for this evening, so she got up and turned off the stove, then sat back down in her chair, defeated.

I walked over to hug her and we both heard my stomach grumble. We all went to bed that night without dinner. The next morning at school I had a dizzy spell, with little lights shining and blinking in front of my eyes. I would later learn this was a sign of malnutrition. I look back on those years and realize how all of this took a heavy toll on my mother. I still think she died from a broken heart. The doctors called it "cerebral hemorrhage" or bleeding inside the brain.

There were many more nights like that last one, and they signaled to my mother her failure. Our friends in the neighborhood stopped coming around because they knew she didn't have food in the house, and even the grocery store clerks who loved to flirt with her wouldn't even send her a small bag of food.

Why was she so hard on herself? Who could have done any better under those conditions? She did not understand that no other mother of twelve living on welfare could have done any better. But she believed that she should be able to feed her family at least once a day. She sometimes made a bet on the number to win some money. If she hit a number she could buy enough food to last a month. And at first, she won, but making the bet became part of the problem. Just like me many years later, she began to depend on that bet. And when her numbers stopped coming in, she started to feel defeated.

One of my last memories of my mother involved her suffering a nervous breakdown when I was eleven years old. As I was leaving for school, I noticed that she was sitting on the couch and staring at the wall. I called out to her and she didn't respond—her eyes were completely blank. She tried to speak, just a gasping breath. She sat there, in her light blue nightgown. That was the first time I ever saw a person completely catatonic.

Thank God she was home with us and not out with some man, I was thinking. She seemed like a robot. I told her to follow me and I touched her hand, and without even questioning me she followed me right out the door. I brought her to our next-door neighbor, Lucy. I explained that something was wrong with my mother. Lucy knew exactly what to do. She took my mom into her living room and told me to go back to my apartment. I then went off to my sixth-grade class.

The ambulance arrived to pick up my mother, and she was in the hospital for about a week. When she came home, she was almost herself again, but I noticed that she was not as alert as she had been. Also, she didn't sing in the kitchen anymore, and I hardly saw her smile ever again.

That next month was my mother's fortieth birthday and she invited some neighbors to the house. I had saved up my money and bought a camera, and that day I took the only picture that I have of my mother. She died four months later. She decided to share one last experience with me the month before she died, and that experience would haunt me for the next five decades.

LADY BIRMINGHAM

My mother Ruth was born in 1929, the youngest of five, in Birmingham, Alabama. In Birmingham, she saw a young man hung from a tree, and she was well aware that a young girl like herself was a target for rape. My uncle Richard, her older brother, tried to protect her, but she knew she wouldn't be safe in Alabama forever. So she came to New York at the tender age of seventeen to escape Jim Crow and racism.

Millions of people watched on television as President Kennedy made his first speech regarding the need for a civil rights bill in 1963. He had watched as black people were attacked by police dogs and set on by fire hoses. So, he made that speech, and I concluded that his assassination was in fact "revenge for Birmingham." So despite all of the conspiracy theories, I solved the big puzzle during my time as a homeless man reading books in a public library.

My mother had a wonderful voice and she sang in the church choir. Her favorite singer was Mahalia Jackson, and on Sunday mornings, I could often hear my mother singing one of Ms. Jackson's famous hymns, "Precious Lord, take my hand. "Precious Lord, Take my hand, lead me on, let me stand" My mother was just over five feet tall and walked with this kind of swagger. Her smile lit up the entire room. Her laugh was infectious. She had a beautiful chestnut brown complexion, and when she spoke she often kept one hand on her hip.

In short, my mother was very attractive, and I saw a lot of men react to her as she walked down the street. They would whistle and try to get her attention, and she would smile and keep walking. Sadly, she just didn't have much luck with relationships. Her first husband was a man named Lester Lewis. They had a son, Harold, and a daughter, Barbara, but that marriage ended after only two years.

Then she met and married a man named Frank Williams. I was given his last name; however, I've always known that Frank was not my father because he was serving time in prison for murder when I was born.

I remember him in his workmen's clothes: a wool shirt, dark jeans, and a brown cap. He was a truck driver so he was often gone for weeks or months. He never smiled. He reeked of sweat. He was ebony black and often spoke while grinding his teeth. His eyes filled with anger.

I'm certain that my mother's life with Frank Williams was horrible. He was a bitter and angry man. She told me once about the afternoon she watched him kill his best friend in our kitchen. She described, "They were having some argument about money, and Frank grabbed a knife from the table, and turned quickly, and rammed the knife into the top of the other man's head. I saw the point of the knife come out the other side." He looked at her with deep piercing bloodshot eyes. She felt pure evil. She screamed. He turned away and ran out the door. She looked at a dead man on the floor in her kitchen. She cried. She called the police. He was arrested later that night. The marriage was over.

Why did my mother marry such a man, a big blurry man, very rough, when she could have married anyone else? Some people believe that attractive women sometimes marry unattractive men based on some weird belief about loyalty. I never understood why my mom settled for this type of man. He was always in trouble, and he was always broke. He looked a bit like the boxer Sonny Liston, dark and intimidating with big hands and a big nose, and he had a quick temper that matched his looks. My brother Richard told me about a fight he witnessed at the local bar while spending some father-and-son-time with Frank. The fight involved a card game and ended with a man shot. Frank Williams got into an argument with one of the other players, he took out a gun and shot the man in the chest right on the spot. Frank finished his drink and calmly walked out of the bar. Richard was stunned. He could never shake that memory, ever.

My mother did not have another relationship for the five years after I was born. I think it was because she was waiting for a certain man to return, who unfortunately never did come back. Perhaps for the second time in her life she had fallen in love. And I like to imagine that the man she fell in love with was my father. I used to call him her Mystery Man. It would take me another five decades, and a DNA test to learn his identity.

But of course, life was hard for her as a single mother, so soon there were other men on and off the scene.

My mother was unlucky in so many ways, but especially in her relationships. All of her romantic relationships were disasters. Most of the men she got involved with were physically abusive. However, these men would learn very quickly that it was not wise to abuse a woman who had with her a football team. My older brothers were well-built young men—Richard at age 16, Gary at 15, and Frank at 14—who could tackle any man and get him off his feet. My assignment, at age 12 was to be the "pitbull." Once the man was down, my job was to sink my teeth into his ankles. Gary was proud that I always did such a good job when we had to take down some creep.

So you can just imagine this poor fool who had just tried to slap my mother: now he has four boys on him, three that hit him from the top, and one little "pitbull" biting his ankles. It was a mess, and the man would quickly leave and not return.

But once or twice the same man would come back and have a repeat of the same experience. We called one of my stepfathers Mr. Ace. He was a very dark black man, a scary-looking guy, with big hands and an angry face. Despite the many fights, he came back from time to time.

In between those visits my mother kept getting pregnant. She had six more children after me, each one year apart. I think my mother was so fertile that some men could just look hard at her and she would get pregnant. But for most of the time that I remember, she was alone with us, her children.

I admit I was a mama's boy. I was at her side every minute of the day to do whatever she needed me to do. She was also a very clever lady. When no one else was around, she would tell me in my ear, "You're my favorite son." The next day, though, she would tell the same thing to Gary. Of course, no one was there to hear it except Gary. Then the next day she would tell Frank he was the favorite, though I am not sure that Frank ever believed her. I don't know that she ever said this to my brother Richard, though he claims that she did. So, for the most part, we were doing anything to please her.

At times my mother had to discipline us. She would beat us with a belt or a tree switch. Sometimes she let us choose which one. My brothers tended to select the belt. As you can imagine, I had trouble choosing either one! Instead, I would fall on the floor crying and convulsing. I could even produce real tears.

My mother would look at me and shake her head, saying, "After all of that I don't think I will give you a beating, but I really should give you an Academy Award for that performance." She laughed at me. I thought, Great! I just avoided a serious beating. Maybe I should become an actor.

I did my best to be a good son. I always did my chores. I walked our dog. King was part German-Shepherd and loved to run in the park. Sometimes I would lose track of time and come back hours later, and then my mother would scold me for being late and for not taking care of other chores. That was one reason I was so angry at her the night before she died. What 12-year-old kid did not get angry at his mom, and say something horrible? I was still her right-hand man and gave her very little grief.

However, not all of us gave her little grief. My brother Richard was in trouble all the time and was often brought home by a police officer. I used to joke around and call him "Spider-Man" because I would see him climbing in and out of other peoples' apartments. I think he fancied himself a second-story man.

One time when Richard was brought home, my mother told the police officer to give him a beating. I stood by the edge of the stairs and listened as the officer took off his belt and began hitting Richard viciously. Can you imagine if that happened today? However, back in 1969, times were different. It was not unusual for a frustrated mother to tell a police officer, "Give my son a good beating."

I've wondered if those beatings explain why my brother Richard chose the path he did. By the time he was twenty-five years old, he had been arrested two dozen times. I struggled to see how I fit in with my older brothers because Richard was really rough and Gary was simply dangerous. Frank just wanted to follow his older brothers. Honestly, so did I, which is to be expected.

I wanted to be like my older brothers. I wanted to be a gangster, I wanted to be a tough guy. The first time I watched The Godfather, I tried to relate that movie to my family. I fantasized that I was "Don Michael," the mastermind, and my brothers were the muscle. Gary at age fifteen already had a body like Marvelous Marvin Hagler, and Richard at sixteen looked like a young Rubin "Hurricane" Carter. Together we were a unit, and we were in the protection business. My brothers protected me, and our number one priority was to protect our mother.

But I was very different from my older brothers, more sensitive, a bit of a wimp. Richard would make fun of me for being too sensitive at times. He would say, "Why are you crying? You are just a little wimp. Stop it." One time, while we were walking on our block, my brothers and I saw a drunk woman climb out too far on her fire escape and fall five stories to the ground. I closed my eyes before she hit the concrete. Richard watched the whole thing and he didn't even blink. He wanted to take a closer look. I did not. Instead, I walked across the street into the neighborhood church, St. Pius. I decided to pray for that woman. The old lady died.

I also had a part-time job at Fred's Pharmacy, from which I brought home a paycheck every week. My mother had gotten me this job by telling Fred that I was fourteen, even though I was just eleven at the time. Despite having older brothers, I was the only one who had a job. I earned $25 a week. The rent for our cramped, four-bedroom apartment was $85 a month, so I was actually paying the rent for the twelve of us.

Like any young boy, I sometimes got angry at my mom simply because she's a figure of authority. The night before she died, I went to bed angry at her because I felt that she didn't appreciate me and all the hard work I did for the family. In my frustration, I did not give her a kiss goodnight.

The next morning, I did not kiss my mother on her cheek before walking out the door to go to school. I always kissed her before leaving for school. But I was still upset with her. I did smile at her before I left. I said; "Ma, after school, I'm going to Mr. Fred's Pharmacy for a few hours, and then I'll come right home, okay Ma?"

She looked at me and said she didn't feel too good. She said she might go see the doctor at Lincoln Hospital. I said "Ok, ma" It seemed that she was always going to the doctor, so I did not think too much about it. Then, I walked out of the door. That was the last time I talked to my mother. I'm still haunted about what may have happened after I left, imagining what her last moments were like. I loved my mother, I worshiped her, and I miss her even now. I suspect that anxiety, stress, and depression killed my mother. Yet I still want to know whether she got to the hospital after all. Did she get a doctor to look at her? What happened before she died?

I only know that my brother Gary arrived at my classroom later that morning. He attended Clark Junior High. So it was strange that he would be standing at the front door of my class.

He looked at me with the saddest eyes and said in a dry voice, "Mommy died today."

I was filled with remorse and shame. I felt some responsibility because of my anger the night before. I wanted to tell her I was sorry for being angry. I wished I had given her a hug and a kiss that morning before I left. I wished I had said sorry for the terrible thing I had said the night before. Instead, she died. I never got to say, "I am sorry for being angry at you." I often wondered, What do I do with this pain?

Our mother was the glue that held the whole puzzle together. Once she was taken away, the family collapsed.

I ended up in the group, along with Frank. The rest of my siblings were scattered in all directions. My brother Gerald was adopted by a Jewish family and they changed his name. Nat, Juan, and Gregory were placed in various foster homes as far away as Rhinecliff, New York, and Susan and Ruth were placed in a group home in Staten Island. I was left for last. However, before the group home, a sweet lady in the building decided to foster me. Her name was Carmen Martinez. Her daughter Mercedes, who would become my foster sister, loved the idea of having a little brother. She convinced her mother to take me in.

Mercedes was a great foster sister and a good friend. However, the arrangement did not work out. I could not accept anyone taking the place of my mother and I began to build up a deep resentment against anyone who tried to take her place.

So, my next stop was the Richmond Hill Group Home for Boys in South Ozone Park, Queens. The people in the South Ozone neighborhood did not exactly welcome the boys of the Richmond Hill Group Home. They considered us a group of outcasts, a gang of freaks. We were creatures with no mothers or fathers. They believed that we would bring down the quality of the neighborhood and the value of their property. The reaction of the neighborhood influenced the dynamics within the group home, and strangely it unified us into a group, the way soldiers in a war unite against an enemy.

I was one of the first twelve boys. First, there were the three McDonald brothers. They were white. Jimmy looked a lot like the actor James Dean. There was also a Puerto Rican boy at the house. Carlos, who looked like the singer Marc Anthony. All the other boys were black like me. We were all roughly the same age, between twelve and fifteen years old. Even though we had different backgrounds, though, we were often unified. We were no longer black or white. We were just "the homeboys." There was always some jealousy among some of the boys.

I did not have a good feeling about the group home staff, and it was during my early years there I began picking up some bad habits. I already knew that I had a problem with authority. That feeling only got worse once I met the so-called "house parents." I said to myself, "You got to be kidding me."

Mr. Morales, a Puerto Rican man who looked a lot like the Panamanian boxer Roberto Durán, was about twenty-two years old. He was not well-liked by the boys. However, Mr. Harris, who resembled the TV and movie actor Robert Hooks, was different. Mr. Harris only had one arm, and the boys called him Mr. Hook. Yet, he seemed to really care about the boys. His wife, Mrs. Harris, was also a great cook. Mr. and Mrs. Harris were good people, they treated us well, and it was unfortunate they did not stay longer. The problem was the other so-called house parent. For example, Morales spent most of the day hanging out upstairs in the private room smoking weed.

I hated the place, especially Mr. Morales because I thought he was a fake. He criticized the boys for drinking cheap wine, and yet he invited young girls up to his room to smoke marijuana. I could stand by Mr. Morales' door and get a pretty good contact high. Whoever his supplier was, he had some good stuff. However, nobody reported him to social services.

Then, Mr. Lorenzo Brown arrived. He eventually was hated by every single boy in the group home except me. Mr. Brown was an alcoholic who could often be found passed out, piss drunk, in the living room. He had a very bad body odor. We made fun of him about that. He would always speak while clenching his teeth. He was always quick to punish the boys. Again, no one ever called social services. But I liked Mr. Brown because the Mother's Day after my mom passed away, I told him I wanted to go to the cemetery to put flowers on my mother's grave, and he took me.

Despite pouring rain that day, we made the two-and-a-half-hour trip. Unfortunately, I had given him the name of the wrong cemetery and we ended up at St. Raymond Cemetery instead of Ferncliff Cemetery, nearly twenty miles away. I remember that the flowers I brought wilted in my hands and my feet were soaked from the rain. Yet Mr. Brown was nice enough to try to make that trip, and for that, he earned my respect.

Another "house parent," Juan Casiano, turned out to be a drug dealer. Ironically, before his time was up at the Richmond Hill home, he had me arrested for possession of marijuana. I had gotten in a fight with one of the other boys in the home, and I pulled out a bb gun. I was once again doing my best to play the tough guy. The bb gun looked real. Casiano arrived with the police to search my room. They didn't find the gun, but they did find five small packets of marijuana. I was arrested and taken to jail. I was sixteen years old.

Spending that first night in jail, I realized how different I was from my older brothers. Jail was not the place for me. I spent that whole night paralyzed with fear, and I decided that if I ever got out of that cell, I would make sure that I never found myself in jail again. I never did.

There was a family a few blocks from the group home who knew me and wanted to help me. I was taken there by Melva, who became my sister. And, then I met Ms. Mary Alice James, and she would become my second mother. She wanted to help me, but I could hear the streets calling me. However, years later she was a big part of my recovery. So, that day I went to jail, Mary showed up with an attorney to get me out of jail. She did not have the money for a lawyer, so she took out a loan. I carefully watched how the attorney managed the situation and was fascinated. That experience stuck with me and I did my best not to end up in handcuffs again. It planted a seed in my mind, I now wanted to be a lawyer.

Some months later another "house parent" arrived: Henry Hank. Mr. Hank was once a professional boxer, a middleweight contender for a title. I immediately despised him. Mr. Hank liked to use the boys in the home as punching bags, and a few of the boys got it bad. It was as if Mr. Hank was flashing back to when he was in the ring. Once, he hit Jeff with a hard blow, I remember his face, grazed eyes, tightened jaw, gulping breaths. The sweat dripping from his black face. I could see that Jeff was hurt, and fell on the floor. Henry Hank walked away. I believed that he still wanted to land that knockout blow. He never actually knocked out any of the boys, but he came close a few times. Hank was not just into punishment, his thing was torture. He seemed to enjoy locking me in a small bathroom in the basement. I called it "the box". The boys all agreed, this was a strange way to run a group home. Yet still, no one made that phone call to social services.

Then there was James Brendon, twenty-two years old. He was in my view the worst of all the group home parents. It was because of him that I took to the streets, and never looked back. Of all the boys in the home, he hated me the most. My defiant attitude toward authority earned his pure contempt. So he came up with a plan. He told one of the other boys to invite me into the basement to smoke some marijuana. When I started smoking the joint, the other boy went to the bathroom. Bruno came up behind me and hit me with a chair. I was 5'7", and about 130 pounds. Bruno was six feet and 240 pounds. He then started kicking and stomping on me. He gave me one of the worst beatings I ever experienced in my life. The beating was brutal.

He reeked of body odor, sweat pouring from his forehead, and blood spilled from my mouth. He cursed under his foul breath "so you're still a proud little nigger?" That was my last day in the group home.

I never told Richard or Gary about the beating because they would have made sure that James Brendon disappeared from the face of the earth. Even though at the moment I wanted revenge, I also sensed that I would regret it years later. I understood that I could cause a person's death. Like Don Michael. So, I never told them. I didn't want that on my conscience. To me, that is real power, when you can cause harm, and have a good reason, and yet, decide against making that call.

Surprisingly, another decent couple was hired by the home at one point, a husband-and-wife team, Mr. and Mrs. Huntley Burke. They were from Kingston, Jamaica, and were the type of house parents that provided us, a sense of normalcy. However, they were not with us very long either, and the different sets of so-called house parents or counselors continued like a revolving door.

Those last few months, I was constantly in disputes with the counselors. I would sometimes spend weeks in solitary confinement, which involved being locked in my small room in the basement. Any violation could land you in trouble. For example, gambling was not allowed. However, it did not take me very long to begin organizing dice games in the basement for all the boys on allowance day.

My other big escape was the movies.

When I won money, I would go to the movie theater on Jamaica Avenue. I saw The Godfather several times there. Another time, one of the other boys gave me a pill called "THC" to take before going to the movies. It was a powerful drug. Unfortunately, I was going to see The Exorcist. This turned out to not be a good experience.

I also saw a movie called The Sting, starring Paul Newman and Robert Redford. I fell in love with that movie and returned many times to watch it again. I was so impressed that I decided to set up my sting operation. It took some careful planning. I stole all the air-conditioners from the group home at 3 a.m. while everyone was asleep in their beds.

However, I lost all the money in a dice game that weekend.

At the group home, I started to lose to the guys in the dice games, which drove me to chase the money. We were given a weekly allowance of $10. For me, my gambling had priority over everything. And even as I was losing, I was still trying to impress the other boys.

My grades began to plummet as I lost interest in school by the age of seventeen. I was never in class; instead, I hosted a dice game in the boy's bathroom. I even resigned from St. Theresa's CYO basketball team, which was incredible considering that getting picked for the team had been one of my proudest moments. I remember how the boys in the group home would not pick me to play in the pick-up games on the street. Yet, I was the only boy in the group home to be selected to play for St. Theresa's basketball team that summer.

I had turned 14 that summer, and making the basketball team was a big deal. All of the boys attended the first game. To the shock of everyone, I was selected as one of the starting five-as the shooting guard. I scored 20 points in that game. The guys were dumbfounded. I walked home wearing my number 9 jersey. The next day, the guys still did not select me to play in the pick-up game on the street. This time I just laughed at them and walked away. I understood envy. It's a bitch. So, it was beyond belief that I would give up my jersey, and quit the team. However, it seemed that I found something more important.

I was soon in trouble with school and the group home's counselors were under pressure about my grades. I did not care because I knew I was about to hit the streets. They suggested I transfer to another school. I had reached the point where I could no longer tolerate living in a group home, and I knew that I was not to be there long. I could no longer live under the authority of the so-called "house parents". They were a bunch of hypocrites in my view. I was also always getting into fights with the other boys. I was constantly in solitary confinement. Then that last beating at the hands of Brendon. It was time to go. I decided to hit the streets and try to make it on my own. Even now, fifty years later, I think if I saw him today, I would feel the anger.

I did have one last time to talk with someone who cared. No one seemed to understand my problems like Mary Alice James. My other mother. However, I did not tell her what life was really like in the group home. And, I could feel the streets calling me in a very strong way.

When I first arrived at the home of Ms. Mary Alice James, I sensed that she was different from anyone that I had ever met. Even my mom Ruth, did not understand me like Mary. We just clicked, maybe because she told me from the beginning, "I can never replace your mother, and I never will. But I'll do the best I can to be somebody in your life who can help you."

With those simple words, I found my second mom. Mary Alice James was born in 1931 and had come to New York from South Carolina, where she had worked in the cotton fields. She was a single mother of three and worked for the MTA as a token booth clerk. Ironically, she loved the racetrack and the horses. It's funny, when I look at my life as a whole, that from one mother I picked up the love of card games and the numbers, and from another, I picked up a love of horse racing.

Mary Alice wanted so much to help me. She even tried to adopt me and had spoken to a lawyer about getting me out of the group home. But it was too late. I had spent five long years in the group home, and my resentment and anger had continued to build up. I also had my first winning streak during that time, and I had begun to believe that gambling was my answer.

I felt that Mary had her hands full caring for her children Charles, Ronnie, and Melva. I felt that I would only be a burden. I could feel it was time to move on. It was time for me to go. So, one night I was gone.

THE EMPTY SUITCASE

The year before I left the group home I finally arranged a meeting with social services. Above all, my mind was filled with questions for the social workers about my family. I didn't understand how someone's family could just be taken away, and I needed to know what had happened to my younger siblings. I thought it was wrong to move families around and change their names. I didn't want my younger brothers and sisters to meet one day and not know that they were family, and maybe even get married. That, to me, was a nightmare.

As far as I knew, Richard and Gary were both in jail, and it was still a mystery to me about how to begin to locate my younger brothers and sisters. By chance, on a very hot day in June of 1973, I ran into my older sister Barbara on the corner of Rockaway Boulevard in Queens. When I first saw Barbara, I was mesmerized. She was the spitting image of our mother Ruth. Some people had said they looked like twins. Even Barbara's mannerisms were just like my mother's. Seeing her standing in the grocery store was like looking at a reincarnation.

For some reason, my mother and my sister had a very turbulent relationship, likely because they were both such strong-willed people. Now, Barbara was married and living with her husband Herbie in a beautiful home near Rockaway Boulevard. At age twenty-six, she was the oldest living member of the family. Her daughter Christine was about six years old at the time.

I confided in Barbara that I could not find our younger siblings, and I hoped that she could help arrange a family reunion. I met with a social worker. I was not having much success with the social workers. She agreed to get involved, and so I warned her about the problems with social services. But, she found a way to make it happen. It was one of the happiest days of my young life when I saw my family for that first reunion.

It was near the end of 1973 and a warm day. Barbara lived with her in-laws in a nice house, with a large backyard. The van arrived with my brothers and sisters. I noticed that Susan and Ruth were so much taller than I remembered. Nathaniel had gained some weight. Gerald was wearing glasses. Juan was still as skinny as ever.

My youngest brother, Gregory, was very quiet the whole time. It felt so good to see them again, and I was already planning the next visit.

Soon I learned more about the exact whereabouts of my older brothers. I received letters from Richard and Gary from a place called Riker's Island. That was the start of another journey that would continue for some thirty-eight years. I would visit places called Attica, Comstock, and Clinton Correctional.

I visited places like Auburn State Prison and Greenhaven Prison and so many others that I don't remember the names anymore. Before I turned eighteen, I needed someone to take me to visit my brothers. The trip was usually a ten- or twelve-hour bus ride. It was a strange feeling traveling to the prisons, like visiting another world.

Family members visiting their incarcerated kin took a midnight bus and arrived at the prison at about 8 a.m. the next day. The bus made a few stops along the way so that passengers could use the restroom and maybe get a snack to eat. I noticed that on these buses were predominantly women and children. And they knew the drill. They knew where to get off the bus to get items to bring to the prison. I was an idiot in the beginning. I showed up empty-handed, thinking my brothers would be happy to just see me. They were expecting a food package.

However, if I had a little money left over from the dice game, I would leave some in their commissary.

Mostly I visited Gary and Richard. Richard did not seem able to stay out of jail. When I visited him, he always told me the same story. He would say, "I didn't do it, Mike! The system is corrupt, the system is racist, it was the system that killed our mother!" I would wonder, what system?

He might explain, "They got me on some trumped-up charge and said that I robbed, and beat up some white man," He told me that the authorities took him into a room and beat him with a rubber hose, giving him a worse beating than even the one from the cop in the South Bronx.

It's not easy to imagine this beating, but just go back and look at the Rodney King video. That was similar to what happened to him. These cops told Richard, "If we want to, we can kill you. Oh yes, we can, because any nigger who ends up dead *should* be dead."

I listened to my brother's stories and looked at his face. His jaw grinding as he spoke, and his eyes turned a dark red. It was a look of revenge. I could see that rehabilitation wasn't working at all. Richard would leave prison after a few years, and within weeks he would be on his way back to prison again, this time convicted of murder in the first degree.

I remember the trial, and I remember the judge who passed the sentence on him. The judge accused my brother of being a coldhearted murderer. I heard lawyers talking about "a life sentence," "three-time loser," and "career criminal." Richard was sentenced to twenty-five years to life for first-degree murder.

I left the courthouse that day thinking that my brother would never be a free man again. I was sure that he would die in prison. Somehow, twenty-five years and several appeals later, things changed. By the grace of God, he survived all those years in prison and walked out a free man. But that part of the story I'll talk about later on.

My brother Frank also spent some time on Riker's Island, but once he was released, he decided to stay out of trouble for a while. Unfortunately, he died at age 37, from drug abuse.

So I finally left the Richmond Hill Group Home for Boys when I was just seventeen. I didn't have a job, so I gambled to survive. In the beginning, it seemed easy. I could win money in card games, in dice games, or at any of the underground casinos that were set up all over the city.

These clubs looked like closed storefronts from the outside. A patron could get in by knocking on the door and, of course, knowing the password. I also made trips to the Belmont and Aqueduct racetracks. They didn't bother to check your age or for identification. At the race track, I pay my two bucks, and walk in the door, to paradise. At that moment, I felt excited. All of my worries seemed to vanish.

It was during my times visiting the racetracks that it became apparent that I suffered from a gambling addiction. I could stay up all night reading my racing form before going to the off-track betting office, or the OTB, and making my bets. I knew that I had all the winners for that day. I might only have about ten dollars in my pocket, but all I needed was to win the first race. I knew I would have a *pile* of money before the last race.

I would even arrive early to the track so that I could get some sleep. I would arrive at eight in the morning when the doors opened, then find a bench and sleep until the first race. The racetrack trumpet was my alarm clock. I could have used my last few dollars to rent a room; however, that was my "gambling money," so in my mind it made more sense to sleep on the train, make a big win at the racetrack, then book a room at the Plaza Hotel. That was my brilliant plan.

Some days I won money, but most days I lost. Sometimes I did not even last until the third race before I was broke again. Not having a steady place to sleep also became a problem. I needed to get off the street because winter was around the corner.

In 1975, I arrived in Harlem to open arms. Gary was out of jail and thrilled to see me. He flashed that fifty-dollar smile. The apartment was small, with a bedroom, living room, kitchen, and a small bathroom, and had barely any furniture, just a few chairs, a sofa bed, and a mattress. The apartment also had neither heat nor electricity. Instead, we used candles. I sometimes dragged the mattress into the kitchen and turned on the stove to keep warm during the night.

But, I had a key, and for now, this was home. Gary somehow did not mention that his rent was seriously past due. I would find out for myself after living with him for only a few months.

Soon, Gary went missing. I still lived in the apartment. I arrived home one night after a long night at the dice game and I fell into a deep sleep. Early the next morning, I heard a key, then the opening of the door. I was excited, as I believed it was Gary coming home. However, when I went I looked up, no Gary, I instead saw two white men and a white woman coming in. One of the men was a city marshal, and he had a gun. Something was wrong.

The white lady told me, "We're repossessing this apartment because the rent has not been paid in thirteen months. Padlocks are going on the door right now. You have ten minutes to leave—take only what you can carry." This was my introduction to the world of homelessness.

Once I got over the shock of finding myself evicted, I tried to make a plan. I was certain I could make a score at the dice game later that night. Then I would return and collect some of my things from the dry cleaners. This, by the way, never happened. I lost badly at that dice game, and I ended up with only the clothes I was wearing and the few items inside my suitcase. It would be six months before I had another change of clothes or somewhere to sleep other than the subway.

I tried to sleep in an abandoned building. The doors were broken and had no locks, the pipes had been stripped, there was no running water, and it was very dark. But, there was still a couch and a mattress inside, and it seemed an okay place for me to get by for the night. I slept and dreamed about the racetrack. A few times the noise from the bar next door woke me up.

The people were talking loudly and clinking their glasses together. Frank Sinatra was singing "New York, New York" on the jukebox. Those folks had no idea that a man was sleeping in this abandoned apartment next door.

I muttered a prayer under my breath. *Lord, get me out of here, please, in the name of Jesus, help me.*

After a long while, the noise from the bar died down and I fell back to sleep. Then, a short while later, I had awakened again. A strange sensation covered my chest. Rats were crawling all over me and the couch I was sleeping on. Each one was the weight of a small kitten. I was not brave about it, and yelled, I jumped up, started throwing things, and quickly reached for my suitcase.

I got out of that building right away and took to the subways again. Now I understood why people don't sleep in abandoned buildings. I would not sleep in a dark room for a very long time after that.

I felt that I had to find Gary. Asking around the neighborhood, I heard that he was somewhere in Brooklyn. I asked, "How do I get to Brooklyn?"

"Take that number five train over there to 14th Street, and take the L train to Brooklyn. I'm not sure what stop you should get off at, try Morgan Avenue."

With that little bit of information, I went off to find my brother. I called the social worker again. I wanted to know about my younger brothers and sisters. I think he sensed that I was living on the streets. He told me to go back to the group home. Maybe then try to plan to see your family again. My pride would not let me admit to anyone how bad things had become. I still dreamed of making the big win.

This got me thinking about Aqueduct Racetrack. So the next day I went back to Queens. I studied my racing form very carefully, I did some quick calculations, and I came up with a brilliant plan.

To start, my plan was to win the daily double, which would pay five hundred dollars for a two-dollar bet. From my winnings, I would bet a thousand dollars on the third race, which would pay 30-1, giving me $30,000. *Nice and easy*, I thought.

If I win, then, I would bet the $30,000, yes, the *entire* $30,000, on a horse named Dancing Secret in the fifth race. Based on my calculations, by the seventh race, I would have myself about $480,000. I would be on easy street before the ninth race.

I did see one small problem with my plan. How could I carry that much money out of the racetrack? In my pockets? No, I thought not. So, I emptied my suitcase and brought it with me to the racetrack. That way, after I made my big hit, I could just fill the suitcase with the money and walk out of the track. This was like my mom back in the Bronx boiling water to prepare to cook a meal for the family. You got to think positively. Like my mom would say. If you pray for rain, bring your "umbrella". My empty suitcase was my umbrella. I was dreaming about my next score and was already spending the money in my head.

Most people would doubt that my plan was even close to reality. However, I had studied my racing form very carefully, and in my mind, winning was a lock. I only had $100 bucks in my pocket—so what? After a few winning bets, I would be on my way to a life of leisure. Should I take a room at the Waldorf or the Plaza?

I had been wearing the same clothes for the last few weeks, brown pants and a dark blue shirt, black shoes with holes in the bottom, and a black coat. My hair was a mess, and I had really bad breath. Yet, I could get clean later, no sense using "gambling money" right now. My green-and-blue suitcase was a bit worn, and yet, ready to hold a half-million dollars.

So, I was ready to win. I approached the gate and gave my two-dollar admission ticket to the man at the front. The security guard gave me and my suitcase a strange look. "Are you looking for JFK Airport?" he joked. *What a smartass*, I thought. Out loud, I told him, "Just give me my damn ticket stub."

To my surprise, I did win the first two races. By the third race, I had five hundred dollars. For just a moment, I considered walking out of the racetrack a winner for once. But I had unfinished business, and my racing form still looked very good for the seventh race. I was determined to win that $480,000., and walk out with my suitcase filled with cash.

So, I made the next bet. Then, the announcer shouted Lady Bird, Hard-Fought Battle, Grey Shadow, and Silver Buck take the lead! Now, Grey Shadow, Silver Buck, Lady Bird pass the stands.

My heart pounded in my chest. I thought I was going to faint. The odds on this race were 7-1. If Silver Buck won, I would have $5,000 on my way to filling up my suitcase.

"Heading down the stretch now is Lady Bird and Silver Buck! They're coming to the wire! Lady Bird is on the outside! Silver Buck is on the inside! Ladies and gentlemen, the winner is—"

Had I won??

The two horses, Lady Bird, and Silver Buck crossed the wire at the finish line at the same time, what's called a "photo finish." On the board, the numbers of Silver Buck and Lady Bird flashed simultaneously. I had to wait for the racetrack officials to make a decision.

My heart still pounding in my chest. The suspense mixed exhilaration and panic, it was overwhelming.

So, how did my master plan work out? Not so good. At the end of the day, I could be found standing outside Aqueduct Racetrack, broke, asking passersby, "Anyone want to buy a good used suitcase, really cheap? Anyone?"

This would be the story of my life as a gambler. It was a struggle for me to face reality because the few times that I won money, that gave me juice to keep going. Most folks cannot understand what that feeling is like for the compulsive gambler. It is more powerful than any emotion, even any sexual experience, you can imagine.

Unfortunately, for a compulsive gambler like myself, the chase tends to lead to a bottomless pit. So it goes. After I went broke at the Aqueduct, I was back to sleeping on trains again.

Losing at the track also put me on the search again, back to looking for Gary. But what happened when I found him nearly cost me my life. First, I went back to the dice game and worked as a gofer for that night. I left the game with about ten bucks in my pocket.

The next day, I followed the instructions I had received, and I took the L train to Morgan Avenue. I eventually found the bar where my brother was last seen, a place called the Tiptop Lounge on the corner of Gates and Myrtle Avenue.

Walking into the Tiptop Lounge, the first thing I noticed was the topless dancer on the stage. She reminded me of Jennifer Lopez. The lounge was dimly lit and all the windows were blacked out. The bar was really close to the stage, so I sat right in front and ordered myself a Johnny Walker Black on the rocks. While I waited for my drink, I fantasized about the dancer. "Rapture" by Blondie played on the jukebox.

I handed the bartender a one-dollar bill to pay for the drink—at that time, a drink was only a buck—and mentioned, "Hey, I'm looking for my older brother, the name's Gary, he's about 5'9" and weighs about 190 pounds. Have you seen him around at all?" The bartender smiled and nodded.

"Do you know where I can find him?" I asked.

The bartender replied, "I think you're talking about Gary Dangerous. You look just like him, you must be his little brother. Yeah, you look alike. He was here last night, and he was here earlier today, too. I'm sure he'll be back in a while. I'll try to find you a phone number, but I'm sure he will be back soon."

I turned my attention back to the dancer. As another song played on the jukebox, I leaned over and began to speak softly to her. Barry Manilow crooned, "Her name was Lola//She was a showgirl//With yellow feathers in her hair and dress cut down." The dancer moved her hips in rhythm.

I told her, "I really like watching you dance. Maybe we can have a drink when you get your break. What's your name?" She replied that her name was Porsche, and she'd be done in fifteen minutes. "Sure, we can have a drink," she said. "I'll talk to you in a few."

I was dreaming about taking her to a hotel when out of the corner of my eye I saw the front door start to open.

The light from the open door reflected off the wall, and a man wearing a long, brown raincoat entered the bar. He walked towards me, and I noticed that he was holding something like a long pipe under his raincoat. A split second later, I realized it was a 12-gauge shotgun.

He stepped directly in front of me and pointed the gun at my head. Porsche jumped off the stage and the bartender backed away, but I was in complete shock. I couldn't move! The gunman pointed at me and pulled the trigger—

—but the gun didn't fire!

The man pulled the trigger again and again. Nothing happened. By this point, I had fallen from my chair onto the floor and was on my knees like a man praying. The gunman moved diagonally, shifting the shotgun, still trying to fire. Out of the corner of my eye, I again saw light coming from the open door, and then my brother Gary entered the scene.

The gunman looked to the door and saw Gary, then did a double-take back at me. He had confused me with my older brother.

I loved Gary more than anyone else in my family, yet at that moment I was paralyzed with fear and was livid with a strange kind of anger. I thought, *If you need to kill somebody, then damn it, kill the right person.* A split second later, Gary charged the guy.

I couldn't believe what I was seeing. The gunman saw my brother running towards him, but he still couldn't get his gun to fire. He dropped the gun and bolted into the men's room at the back of the bar. I heard the lock click. Barely pausing, Gary began to pull the bathroom door off its hinges with his bare hands. I was certain that I was about to witness a homicide.

I quickly realized that there was some bad blood, maybe a drug deal that went bad, between my brother and this man. Yet, there I was in the middle of it.

Just as Gary removed the door, we saw the man's foot exiting the open bathroom window. I picked up the shotgun from the floor and saw that the safety was on. That's why it didn't fire. The gunman must have been nervous taking on Gary, or in a bit of a hurry, and he didn't check the safety. If he had, I would've died that night in Brooklyn.

I needed a drink. I gulped down the rest of my scotch, Johnny Walker Black

It didn't help. My hands shook and my feet were cold. My entire body was tight. I had never experienced such fear before, and I still haven't since.

Gary came over to make sure I was alright. "I'm sorry about that," he said. "Believe me, when I find him, he's done." He explained that they had been having a dispute between the two of them for the last few weeks. Now, Gary added this situation to the list of problems between him and the gunman. "No need to tell you what I'll do to him when I find him after what he did to you," Gary promised me. I did not want to know. He then told me to hang outside the Tiptop Lounge for a few minutes while he went across the street to handle some business. "I'll be back," he said as he walked out.

First, I ordered another drink and listened to the jukebox. I was down to my last three dollars and was still feeling paralyzed, unable to speak.

I really needed to talk to my brother. I had been evicted from his place in Harlem.

I had no place to live and no money, and I had been searching for him for four weeks. Now, I had finally found him in a bar in Brooklyn but felt like I had walked into the O.K. Corral. I was slipping into a state of depression. Life was not worth living.

I stepped outside for a cigarette and realized it was getting late. Worse, I realized Gary was nowhere to be found. *Where do I go from here?* I thought. *Where do I sleep tonight?*

My head was spinning. I was feeling down. I could hear the music. I heard Bob Dylan singing on a nearby radio. The words "Like a Rolling Stone" seemed to haunt me. It was like he was singing to me. "How does it feel//To be without a home//A complete unknown//Like a rolling stone?"

I needed to get away from all of this drama. I was feeling hopeless. Life was not worth living. However, first things first. I needed money. I knew that there was always a card game nearby, and I considered that that could be my ticket to a better place. I would need to be the gofer for a few hours just to get a few bucks.

Then I thought for a moment of going back to Queens, maybe back to my old neighborhood. My foster mother, Mary Alice James, was still there, and I was sure that she would help me. Mary James never gave up hope. She later told me that she prayed for me every day, and hoped that I would return one day. Which I finally did. Yet, at that time, I couldn't go back. I could not let her see me this way. It was my pride again. Pride is one of the deadly sins.

However, it was clear that things were not working for me. Gambling had taken over my life and the urge to gamble was all-consuming. I had reached a point where I was not even concerned with my younger brothers and sisters anymore. However, I would soon meet a person who influenced me to move in a different direction. Yet, there were still some real ups and downs ahead.

TAKE THE A TRAIN

By 1977, I had been evicted three more times. When I moved into a place, either into an apartment or a furnished room, the landlord always requested the first and last month's rent payment. By now I recognized that my gambling addiction was controlling my life. I felt sorry for the landlord. I told myself that it was just as well if I paid the first and last month upfront because that "first payment will probably be the last."

I was not deliberately trying to be funny. I was just coming to terms with the facts of my addiction to gambling. I found a room in Queens. The house was owned by a nice Jamaican family. The old lady who owned the house appeared simple. But she was clever. The room was small but comfortable. To me, the house resembled that Norman Bates' house in the movie "Psycho." I came home one night and my key did not work. My things were in the backyard.

When I moved into a furnished room, I soon learned that the process of eviction was much quicker. If I missed two or three weeks of rent, the landlord just changed the locks on the door. More and more I found myself sleeping on the subway. The L line that ran through Canarsie still used the old subway cars with the cushioned seats and they were the most comfortable for sleeping on. On occasion, I camped out on building rooftops. I remembered learning in seventh grade that heat rises, so when it got cold outside I went all the way up to the rooftop exit. My science teachers were correct; it was much warmer upstairs on the roof. However, I remained committed to never sleeping inside any abandoned buildings again.

It was getting warm again. So, I would sleep on the trains more. That year was also the "Summer of Sam," and New York City was in the grip of terror. A maniac named David Berkowitz was going around shooting people, and everybody was scared. The fact that he was shooting white women or white couples did not give much comfort to anyone in my neighborhood. The city was on edge. Everybody was stressed out. I felt the tension everywhere I walked and I noticed many of the usual places shutting down.

Once again, the movie theater was my great escape. That summer I saw *Saturday Night Fever* and *Star Wars.* I preferred movies that had a dark side, and I rarely saw comedies. I bought tickets to see movies called Black Sunday, Close Encounters, The Deep, and Looking for Mr. Goodbar. I liked the movie *Orca.* The main character was a loner like me, so it was my kind of movie. I also became obsessed with a movie called "Taxi driver." Another story about a loner, yet, this time I could really feel a connection to the character in the movie. I was always looking for ways to get money for the movies, and a few times I was able to sneak into the theater. I could get a few dollars as a gofer or as a look-out at the dice game. In the summer, they would sometimes have the dice game in the park. My job was to look out for the cops.

The movie that would change my life, and eventually almost cost me my life, was *The Deer Hunter.* In one scene, a group of men played a game, we called that game "Russian Roulette" They would gamble on life and death with a loaded gun. You put one bullet in, spin the barrel, and pull the trigger. If the gun didn't go off, you won the bet. If the gun did go off, you did not win—obviously. I felt a rush of adrenaline watching that movie.

To add to the drama of the year, New York City experienced a major blackout during the summer. All around me, Brooklyn was in chaos. People broke into stores and burned cars. In the midst of all this, I was still struggling to find a place to sleep for the night. I found a rooftop.

The life of a homeless person is quite challenging. Take my diet, for example. I lived on one meal a day. If I was lucky, I could go to Burger King and order a Whopper and a drink. Most days I had to settle for a slice of pizza and a cup of coffee.

I often panhandled in front of the subway stairs, waiting to see a face that appeared sympathetic. Yet, it is very difficult to panhandle if you are truly homeless. Most people can't possibly understand the level of shame and embarrassment that a homeless person feels every day. I wanted more than anything in the world to be invisible.

When I ride the subways today and see people announcing to the entire train that they are homeless, I think it is pure nonsense. Those folks are fakes. Homelessness destroys your self-esteem, your sense of self-worth.

A truly homeless person's greatest fear is being seen by someone who knew them before they were homeless. So, I find it unlikely that someone who's hit rock bottom would announce their circumstances to a full subway car or draw attention to themselves in that way.

I would just look into the crowd of people. I would wait a long time before I would approach anyone. However, I could hear that noise. It was my stomach. I need something. Coffee. Or, even better. A roll with butter, and coffee. So I looked for sympathetic faces in the crowd and approached a few people. I would say, "Excuse me, sir, can I trouble you for a quarter? I just need a cup of coffee." I do not recall ever approaching a woman. Again, this was all about pride.

Most people simply walked away, and it was not uncommon for me to stand there for three or four hours and collect maybe a dollar or two.

To be homeless and a compulsive gambler was also a strange paradox. It was the ultimate roller coaster ride. On any given day I could be panhandling to get a cup of coffee just a few days after betting and losing hundreds of dollars at a card game. Or, overnight I am having dinner at Beefsteak's Charlies

Every waking moment my mind was consumed by thoughts of gambling. The thing about gambling was the anticipation. We call it "the juice". And, the only thing that mattered to me, was the action. In the heat of the moment, I could forget that I hadn't had a meal that whole day. The feeling was even stronger at the racetrack. The anticipation was even more powerful. The scene was intoxicating. The fresh air, the sound of the crowd, seeing the horses making the clubhouse turn. Once again, I was convinced, *I am home free when my horse comes in.*

But in reality, I would finally learn that there's no such thing as something for nothing. In the end, we always have to pay for whatever it is we accept in life.

So just as quickly, all that glamor would disappear and I would be on the street again. But that was okay. I'd tell myself, with my racing form in hand, "From what I can see, today will be my day, and in a few hours, I can change everything."

This is just a glimpse of the roller coaster ride that was my entire life for many years. However, the depths of my misery were fathomless, as my dreams came crashing down.

Each night in the subway, I spent hours trying to work up the courage to jump in front of the next train. I knew deep down inside me that my life was a mistake.

Most people may not understand the power of chronic depression, anxiety, and stress. We know that almost every holiday season in the city, we hear about someone jumping in front of a moving train. I only hoped I could find the strength to do it myself. At least then I knew I would be with my mom again.

One morning, it had to be three or four AM, I woke up on a subway bench and looked across the track to the other platform. A man was standing on the edge, completely nude. His clothes were folded into a neat pile next to him. Before I could even register what I was seeing, a train roared into the station and the man jumped. It happened in a second. I didn't even have time to yell out. He was killed instantly. After, all I could think about was the pile of folded clothes. What was that about? Why did he fold his clothes? After seeing that, though, I stop having fantasies of jumping in front of a train.

I did my best to shake that memory. However, I could not. I would wake up from a dream, this time thinking about the guy who jumped. I became depressed and knew I needed to get out of this situation. I tried to pray to God. Quickly, though, my mind jumped back to making a big win and getting a room. I still believed that gambling could be the answer to my problems.

Then by the end of 1977, I was on a brief winning streak again. Gambling gave me my identity and the power to solve other people's problems. If someone came to me and needed money to buy food or pay bills, I could reach in my pocket and hand them some money. I could feel important again.

That summer, I was able to contact my older sister Barbara again, and we arranged for another family union. I still had some money from that weekend's dice game in my pocket and was very excited to travel back to South Ozone Park. The reunion was great.

All of my younger brothers and sisters arrived before me. Later, my brother Frank showed up. I had not been able to get in touch with Gary, and Richard was still in jail.

However, I still did not know exactly where or with whom all of my siblings lived. My sisters Susan and Ruth were still in the group home. Nat was in foster care somewhere. Juan and Gregory were in a group home somewhere in upstate New York. Gerald had been adopted and was living with a family in Rochester.

That next day I won over one thousand dollars in a dice game. What does an eighteen-year-old do with a thousand dollars in his pocket? I'll tell you what he does, he goes crazy. I went to Jamaica Avenue and went shopping. It did not take long before I was broke again.

I still did not have a place to live, but I was becoming a bit of a ladies man. I met a woman, about thirty years old, married, who let me sleep in her basement. After her husband left for work each morning, she would come downstairs to bring me food and have sex.

I felt a little nervous at first, knowing that she and her husband were asleep upstairs. I did not sleep much. He didn't know that I was in his home. After a few weeks, I decided it wasn't worth the risk, even though I was experiencing sex in a way I hadn't ever before.

I met another lady, also older, about thirty-five years old, named Toni. She was also married and had five children. I do not know why as a barely legal teenager I was attracted to older women. I started spending time with Toni at her house when her husband was not home. A few times he did arrive home when I was there, but she told him I was her younger sister Paula's boyfriend, and that Paula was running late. The husband did not even question her about me. He would gather his things and leave for work. I would stay and have drinks with Paula during those times.

I managed to keep a little money in my pocket at times, but it was pretty much touch-and-go. The real issue again became finding a steady place to live. It was not possible to find a place to crash each night, and I only knew about three married women. For some reason, I avoided single women, I never had the money to spend on them.

I was a gambler and I seemed to meet unhappy married women a lot. I was also a good talker, and they often laughed at my jokes.

I decided to continue my search for Gary. My brother was always on the move, and I was told he was back in Harlem. I found a whole new world of gambling in Harlem. There were even more underground social clubs than in Brooklyn. I could find action almost anywhere, and for a while, I was still able to win a little money.

Most of the clubs were in places that had once been other things: a convenience store, a furniture outlet, even a barbershop. As a social club, the whole front of the store was blacked out, usually painted a dark color, sometimes with curtains covering the front windows. There were no signs on the outside door or numbers to indicate the address. In some cases, you had to know the password, a special knock on the door, to get in. Even then you were not guaranteed to get inside. Someone on the inside had to take a look at you, and if they didn't recognize you, then no go.

I spent much of my time as a gofer. These clubs always needed a guy to run errands. I ran for coffee and sandwiches for the men who gambled in the card and dice games. The club was open from 6 PM to 6 AM. I was usually one of the first to arrive in the evening. It was often dark when I arrived, and when I left in the morning, it was still dark outside. It was not unusual for me to go weeks at a time without seeing the sun. I started to feel like a vampire. I felt like I understood the undead.

I would sometimes find the courage to call my godfather, Mr. Monty White. I loved my godfather, and I believe he was the first person to make a positive impression on me. He was the first black man that I ever spoke with who appeared to be a professional, and who dressed as a businessman. For a while, I even believed that my godfather was my real father. I heard a rumor that he was in love with my mother and may have had an affair with her after Frank Williams went to prison. I later learned the true identity of my father.

Yet, I wanted to make my godfather proud of me, and so I lied to him about how I was doing in school. I would not tell him that I was sleeping in the streets. He was someone I could hit up for money, but I struggled to tell him the truth about what was happening in my life.

Once again, my pride would not let me confess to my godfather just how bad things were going for me.

Mr. Monty always gave me money. Time and again I used that money to get back into the dice game in Harlem.

I had a brief winning streak and then my luck turned bad again. Rather than stop me, this just added fuel to my fire. I again escaped by watching movies, including *Midnight Express.* It was dark and depressing, yet I got some comfort from watching films like this, so I watched it over and over again.

I also really liked *Heaven Can Wait* with Warren Beatty, and I watched it six times in two days. I saw *Apocalypse Now,* and *Escape from Alcatraz.* I would try to hide out in the movies. These movies made me think about my brother Richard. During his last few years on the streets in the Bronx, he earned the nickname "Alcatraz" because he was one of the most feared guys in the South Bronx.

By 1978, I had fallen into a state of deep denial about my gambling addiction. The feeling of winning and the intoxication of the dream world fuels the gambler within me to continue the chase. The world of the gambler is simple. They want to have just one more winning day, they want to feel on top of the world just one more time, and they'll do anything to make that happen.

I began borrowing money from dangerous people, and I made reckless commitments to pay them back. I made crazy deals with people to borrow money, most were drug dealers. Any person in my situation might borrow money from a loan shark or a drug dealer and request a week or two to pay the money back with interest. However, as a gambler, I could sometimes pay back the loan the very next morning. I was also willing to pay a very high interest rate for money. If I borrowed one hundred dollars, I would agree to pay back one hundred and fifty dollars the next day. What drug dealer wouldn't want to lend me money? They all agreed, I was a stone sucker.

The word was out in the neighborhood. These people thought I was the biggest sucker in the world, but I knew that once I won big I would be laughing at them all the way to the bank.

Unfortunately—and maybe no surprise- things did not quite work out the way I had imagined. I soon found myself heavily in debt, and in a lot of trouble. The word on the street was that I was a "dead man walking." However, I was desperate to recapture my winning streak. I continued going back to the games, and now I started taking trips to Atlantic City.

Atlantic City was a magical place that I hoped would solve all my problems. By now I was struggling with chronic depression on top of all the stress from knowing that so many people had put a price on my head back in my neighborhood. I looked over my shoulder at every turn.

A good friend of mine, Tony Moschetto, owned a glass shop on Wyckoff Avenue. We met on his birthday in a strip club in 1977. We hit it off right away. Tony found out about how bad things were for me and he let me spend the night in his shop. His guard dog barked at me all night and chewed up my hat. Tony's mother found out about that and she told him that I would sleep on the couch the next night.

Tony and I were very close, and he had often invited me into his home to have dinner with his family. They were an old-fashioned Italian family, with his eighty-five-year-old grandmother living downstairs. As I sat having coffee with his mom and dad, I was a little jealous that Tony had that kind of family and all that love in his life, which I never experienced. Yet, he proved himself to be a true friend. One morning his grandmother, who would live to be one hundred years old, touched my face as she woke me up to give me soup. I wondered what this elderly Italian lady, born in 1890, thought about finding this young black man sleeping on her living room couch.

In my mind, Tony was Frank Sinatra and I was Sammy Davis, Jr. We went all over Brooklyn together and did not care if the folks in the bars were all white or all black. Soon, our group included Vinny, Eddie, and Joe. In my mind, we were the new Rat Pack.

He would even invite me to Seneca Bar for drinks. The bar was in his neighborhood, and black people did not drink in Seneca Bar. I walked in to meet Tony, and Sinatra was singing "summer wind" on the junk box. "The summer wind came blowing in from across the sea" The bar looked similar to the bar in the television show "Cheers".

It was like a large circle. There were a few pictures on the brown wooden wall and only one window. Tony walked into the restroom. A guy stepped up to the bar and ordered a drink. He saw me and seemed very annoyed. He looked directly into my face. He said "I hate niggers, that's just how I feel" I did not respond quickly. Then, I said "Yeah, I hate niggers too."

He seemed a bit astonished. Then, after a few seconds. He said, "Yeah, you know, anybody could be a nigger". He looked at the bartender. "I want to buy this man a drink". This time, I said to the bartender "Dewar's white label" I did not order my favorite Johnny Walker Black, no need to rock the boat. Tony walked back up to the bar. "Everything ok, Goombah?" I nodded. Then, Vinny, Eddie, and Joe Sullivan walked in. The Rat Pack was in the house. Each guy greeted me with a handshake, and kiss on the cheek. The guy standing next to me looked around, seemed puzzled, then he quickly finished his drink, and left.

The next day the Rat Pack met back in my neighborhood. I was at the "El Condados" bar on Gates Ave. It was a very popular Latin club. I was watching the dancer when Tony walked in. Tony was concerned about me. A song played on the junk box, "Native New Yorker" Tony smiled when he saw me. "You look like hell, Mike, what's up?" I was still looking at the dancer. "I may have a new job next week". Tony ordered a beer. He knew I was having money problems. He had heard from the drug dealers on the streets, they told him "If we find that nigger, we'll kill him."

Tony knew these guys well and he knew that I was in real trouble. So, he gave me a .38 pistol with five bullets to protect myself. I thanked Tony for the gun. I really did appreciate his help. My first thought was that I could sell the gun and use the money to get into the card game that night. One big win would solve all of my problems. Yet, deep inside, though, I knew that I would fail again. It seemed like a better idea to blow my brains out. I was haunted by the memory of the movie *The Deer Hunter* and the game that was played in it.

See, I had hit rock bottom, and while my hunger for gambling and a chance to recapture the dream world was still very strong, my depression, stress, and anxiety were taking a toll as well. I thought more and more about suicide.

I had no place to sleep and did not tell Tony. I found a warm spot on a rooftop. I had some scotch left in a small bottle.

That night I got a little drunk. So, I played a very dangerous game. Again, I cannot explain how I survived that night. The next morning, I started to sober up. I looked at the gun. I thought about the three angels that my mother once told me about. I wondered if they were with me last night.

There was another night I survived that I can't explain. It was now late December, and the temperature was ten below zero outside, and I was not properly dressed. I wore only a very thin jacket because earlier I had left my coat at one of the clubs and it was gone when I returned. I knew that if I stayed outdoors that night I would not survive. Not even the rooftop was an option. However, I reached out to someone I met while working security. He agreed to let me spend the night on his couch. His name was Claudius Jean or C.J. However, there was a problem, he was moving that day.

C.J. knew I had a gambling problem and wanted to help me. I promised him I would stop gambling and get myself a room the next week because I had found some work as a security guard. But, I had lost that next paycheck in the dice game and was back on the streets. I called C.J. again. The temperature was dangerously low. I saw one homeless man, who I knew would freeze to death. He had taken off his shoes, despite the temperate of minus ten degrees. Finally, I got C.J. on the phone.

He told me he was moving out of his apartment and had no furniture, so there was nowhere for me to sleep. But, he offered me the chair in his kitchen. I accepted. I slept that night sitting in the chair with my head on his kitchen table. The next day I woke up and looked out the window. The morning had cut night's miserable throat. And, it was Christmas Day, I had survived the night. If I had been on the street instead, I know I would've died. I thought about the three angels.

I had come to the point where depression, stress, and anxiety were my constant company in life. We traveled everywhere together. Before long, it would have felt awkward to not have these three companions along for the ride. I was beginning to give up hope of recapturing my dream world.

Yet, in my sleep, it always came back to me. I would wake up hearing a voice tell me to try one more time. *Maybe this time we should go to Las Vegas.*

One day, as I was standing in the Off-Track Betting office (OTB), and I saw a sign advertising help for gambling addictions. I called the number and talked to someone on the phone. I started to finally think about making some changes in my life. It would still take more years and more misery, but I would eventually give up my pursuit of gambling. I would finally realize that I had to give up gambling if I ever wanted to have a life.

However, once you are a compulsive gambler, you are always a compulsive gambler. There is no cure.

However, my first step was getting off the streets. First, I needed to find positive people to talk to about my problems. I became a bit hopeful for the first time in my life, yet, I was not home free. The addiction does not let go without a fight. For me, I was in for the fight of my life.

CHAPTER 2

"I talk to ex-gamblers all the time, and I've learned one very important thing – you are only as sick as the secrets you keep."

Anonymous

CHASING THE DREAM WORLD

It was 1980, and my gambling addiction was even worse. The addiction would lead me to a new reality of what I called "the underworld." However, deep down inside I knew it was time to find a new direction. The world around me was changing. I would now see graffiti everywhere in the subway. In the U.S. election, a man named Ronald Reagan would become the President of the United States. Later that year, a madman by the name of Mark Chapman would shoot and kill John Lennon. I sometimes would hear his music. Lennon seemed to be all about peace, and yet, he died in the streets like a gangster.

Oddly, when I was growing up, all I wanted was to be like my brothers. I wanted to be a gangster. Yet, I knew that I didn't fit in with them. I was not even close. My brothers were real gangbangers, and street fighters. I would jump when I saw my own shadow.

But, I was a good talker.

I could even make a grown man cry by telling my story about losing my mother at such a young age and growing up poor and black in the South Bronx. I would talk about my life in the group home, and living on the streets. Strangers felt so sorry for me that they gave me money, and I got better each time I told my story. Maybe I should have had somebody standing next to me playing the violin.

But the end was near, even I could feel that something was really wrong. I felt like I was cheating myself out of a real life. I would sit in a bar telling people about my life, and the problems of race and poverty. Rarely did I tell anyone the truth about my gambling addiction. It never came up. I knew it was time for something to change, but I wasn't sure how. Maybe I needed to look at the obvious truth staring me in the face. My real problems were not the result of being poor or black. Although racism and poverty are real, my problems resulted from the fact that I was a gambling junkie. My problems had become unmanageable because I was consumed by my addiction to chasing the action.

Even today, it is still a bit of a puzzle. What is gambling? In my mind, the gambler lives inside of all of us because everything in life is a chance. When you walk out the door to go to work, do you know for certain that you're coming home that night?

No. You're taking a gamble. So to me, life is a gamble. The person who works in the real estate office, or the person who works in the barbershop. The lady who buys a lottery ticket, or the lady who opens up a new nail salon. The man who starts a new business. They are all taking their chances. We gamble every day, whether we know it or not. So, why not take a chance in life?

By the end of 1980, my world was falling apart. Yet, I wanted to hear that last loud roar. So, I went to another big dice game in Brooklyn again. This time I was mugged by a man with a gun outside of one of the underground clubs. I had won some money, and he was waiting outside. I had forgotten how quickly the news traveled when money was won in a dice game. It seemed that even when I won, I lost.

I had one more winning streak before the holidays, and then I crashed.

My final winning streak lasted two weeks. One afternoon I picked eight of the nine races at Aqueduct. I felt like I could not lose. The more I won, the more I bet. I dreamed about what I would do when I had time to spend the money.

It turned out that I didn't do much. I felt good while I had that pocket full of money, but the only thing I could think to do was run from one OTB to the next. Then I turned up at a few bars and bought rounds of drinks for everyone. Once again, I played the role of the big shot. Then the winning streak ended, and I realized that I hadn't even taken time to get a new pair of shoes.

A person suffering from gambling addiction is likely to experience three stages. The first stage is the winning stage, the second stage is the losing stage. The final stage is the desperation stage. During the desperation stage, a gambler acts out of denial. Denial is one of the most powerful elements of the crash because it causes a person to act in the same way over and over again and expect different results. In some circles, this is also called insanity. Denial was my most insidious character defect, regardless of whether I was gambling, or drinking. During this final stage, I also found myself sacrificing personal relationships, family relationships, and friendships. I would cash bad checks, lie to family and friends, and would steal anything except a red hot stove.

I became friends with a family in the next building. There, I had met a beautiful young woman named Maria and had fallen head over heels. Maria reminded me of the famous singer Selena. Her family had come to New York from Puerto Rico. I loved Maria's positive attitude and beautiful smile. We wanted to live together. We even talked about getting married. There was one big problem, she had a very brief relationship with a young man, and was expecting a baby. I did not seem to care, I wanted to be with her. I decided to really try to make this work.

I managed to rent a one-bedroom apartment for us, but Maria began to notice that my electricity was repeatedly cut off when she would come to visit me. At first, I was able to explain it away. Soon she noticed other problems like that the phone was cut off, that there was no food in the fridge, or—and this was really bad—that I would tell her I was going out for an hour and not return until the next morning or a few days later.

Finally, she told me she was leaving me. She said, "I can't go on like this, Michael! I love you, I want to be with you, but you must be seeing somebody else! Why else would you not come home at night?"

I argued and promised that there was no one in my life but her. "Maria, please believe me! I don't want you to leave. I'm not involved with another woman. I'm just having a little bit of a rough time right now, but I'll work it out, I promise you—just hang in there with me for a little while longer."

She thought for a second but then shook her head. She told me she was aware of my gambling problem, too. "If there was another woman, that'd be one thing, but the gambling... Well, I don't believe you'll ever give that up, I cannot compete with that."

Then she left. At first, I couldn't believe it. I was really in love with this young lady. For once in my life, I wasn't chasing after a married woman or some topless dancer. I had really thought we could have a life together. But Maria was right. Gambling came first.

I got evicted from that apartment. I went around the neighborhood selling the furniture. Instead of admitting that I was a sick, compulsive gambler, I bragged to people about what a good salesman I was.

I convinced people that I just wanted to get rid of my furniture, just for the hell of it, they all knew better. They all knew that I was very sick.

I also sacrificed relationships with family members. My godfather Mr. Monty had stood by me after my mother died. He loved me like a father would love a son, and I always knew my gambling would disappoint him. I ended up lying to him on his deathbed, a choice I still regret. I told him that I had graduated from high school and that I had been accepted to John Jay College. That was not true. I had dropped out of high school. Later, I would earn my GED.

I even lost my job as a store clerk at the liquor distributor. For a short period, I maintained a job working for a large store, but even the job became an impediment to my availability to gamble.

My main responsibilities were the inventory of the store and mopping floors. Yet, I somehow convinced myself that I was a vital worker. My boss was a man named Herbert Ehrlich, the owner of Ehrlich's Liquors. One day I told him that I was going to quit unless he gave me a raise. I told him someone had offered me another job with more money, and I pointed toward 72nd Street and Broadway. The only place that I knew of on 72nd and Broadway was the OTB.

Mr. Ehrlich looked at me very calmly, and said, "Good luck with that new job, Mike." So I was out of a job—but I didn't care. I now had time to focus on my racing form and pick my horses for the next day.

I wanted one last big win. I wrote bad checks all over town, and the owners of Tony's Bar or the Tiptop Lounge would cash them. I was always amazed that they would, but I guess they must've thought, Why not? This jerk is going to sit around and buy drinks for the topless dancers. The dancers seemed to understand me, and they knew how to undress fast. Which is useful for a compulsive gambler.

So, I wrote checks, then spent most of the money in the bar. I held on to some money to bet at the OTB. Checks took three days to clear, so I could not go back to the bar until I had made good on the check. In my mind, it made sense to cash the check in the bar, buy a few drinks, and keep some of the money to gamble later on.

Then, hopefully, after I won I could go to the bank and deposit before the checks started to bounce. This was a crazy way to finance my gambling.

Sometimes I arrived at Ralph's bar and he called me over to talk. He'd say, "Mike, you wrote a couple of checks last week and they came back from your bank. I need you to make these checks good before the end of the week, or else we're going to have a problem."

I'd reassure him, "Hey Ralph, don't worry about it! The bank teller must've put my deposit into my savings instead of my checking account. I'll have that taken care of by tomorrow."

My stories went on like that over and over again. A landlord would be on the verge of evicting me, but I would tell them that there was no reason to go through with the eviction because I would have the money by 3:30 PM the next day. The landlord was relieved, thinking I must have a family member coming by to help with my rent. What the landlord didn't know was that the reason I wanted to wait until 3:30 PM the next day was that that was the end of the seventh race at Aqueduct. I was banking on a hunch that my horses would come in.

Of course, this was all complete and total insanity. I had so many different schemes and so many different ideas to solve my problems. I even tried to open my own "casino" in the park.

In my case, my denial was as strong as it could be. By this point in my gambling life, I had become a conditioned loser. I had become accustomed to being evicted, too. I was evicted almost every month. One year I moved eleven times. So, I stopped renting apartments of my own and started living in and out of furnished rooms, which expedited the eviction process. I slept more and more on the L train, first for a few days while I was in between apartments, and then for a few weeks, and finally for months at a time. I could go six months without changing my clothes or brushing my teeth.

If you've seen a homeless man in the subway, you know what someone who hasn't had a bath in six months smells like. I was that person. It was important to me that I not be seen by anyone that knew me.

But I needed help and I had nowhere to live. I was embarrassed. As I was about to hit rock bottom, I turned up at Gary's front door. My brother had decided to settle down a bit. He was not working the streets as much. Yet, as soon as I walked in, Gary's wife Ronnie grabbed the Lysol, sprayed the room, and screamed, "He has to leave!" She began spraying the room. I smelled really bad. I had been sleeping in my clothes for months. Gary started to argue with her. I could see a fight was brewing, and I truly did not want to break up my brother's family.

Gary started packing a suitcase, cursing at Ronnie. I looked at Gary and said, "What are you doing?! This makes no sense. We can't both be sleeping on the street!"

He looked at me and said, "This suitcase is for her! She can go live with her sister!"

I was a bit shocked that Gary showed such love for his little brother. But still, I did not want to be the cause of this breakup. I reached in my pocket and took out a key. It was just one of the many keys that I had in my pocket from some room that I had been evicted from. I held up the key and announced, "Calm down, folks, I have a room. See? Here is my key. I do have somewhere to live. I just wanted to come by to visit."

Gary looked at me with his poker face—he knew I was lying, but he said nothing. His wife breathed a sigh of relief and quickly made up with Gary. "You see, honey, he has a place to live. Why are we fighting?"

I turned and walked out the door, feeling sick in my stomach. I had played my last card, and I felt that this time on the streets would be worse than before. It was in the dead of winter, and it had started snowing. I wished that I had at least gotten some food before I headed out because I was really hungry. I walked towards the subway and I stood there for a few hours panhandling to get loose change. I finally got about a dollar and fifty cents and bought a hot coffee and a few buttered rolls.

I went back to the subway and jumped over the turnstile to get on the train. I headed to a place where no one would bother me, where I could keep warm and hide, to the library on 42nd Street and Fifth Avenue.

The New York Public Library is one of the largest buildings I've ever seen. Back then, it was not like it is today, with all the security and cameras monitoring people coming in and out. Back then I could walk in and not really be noticed by anyone. I could go upstairs and find an area that was warm and comfortable, and I could often stay in the library for hours and hours. Sometimes I even napped. I was rarely ever bothered, though once in a while a security guard would find me hiding in a corner and tell me to leave.

But I could not always hide in the library. I was becoming more and more depressed and anxious. I spent more of my days searching through the trash cans in the OTB for uncashed tickets because sometimes winners did not realize that they were due a refund. If I found a ticket that I could cash in, I used the money to buy breakfast.

It was becoming more difficult to get a meal each day. It was becoming more and more difficult to find a place to sleep at night. Most nights I turned up at the underground social club just to watch the other men play poker and dice. I still looked for any chance to get into the action, but my main role there was to be the gofer for the men. I was always able to scrape up two or three dollars that way.

The social club was predominantly Puerto Rican, but most of the big bettors were white. The guy who operated the social club was nicknamed "Country Sausage." I thought he looked a little bit like the actor Luis Guzmán. One of the big bettors, we call them the "the whales," was a guy we called "Mafioso" because he always wore a white fedora and smoked a cigar. I think his real name was Nick. He looked like Cesar Romero, who played the Joker on the old Batman TV show.

The big bettors, including Country Sausage, were all wrong bettors. They always bet the dice would lose. And they depended on suckers like me who were right bettors. However, I stood out from all the other right bettors, because the other right bettors would arrive with money, and every night go home broke. I was the only right bettor who was broke *all the time.*

The club was next door to a cafe called Joe and Mary's Italian-American Restaurant on Knickerbocker Avenue and Jefferson Street. Some people may remember Joe and Mary's as the place where the Mafia kingpin Carmine Galante was assassinated. The social club was the size of three railroad cars. It was dimly lit and all the windows were blacked out. There were no signs on the door and the door was always locked, so even when you knocked you were never sure that anyone would let you in. But, the Spanish music playing inside could be heard from the outside. The songs of Hector Lavoe and Willie Colon were playing on the jukebox.

There were almost no black players at the game, and nobody spoke "English." It was more like a broken Spanish mixed with English. After a few months, I too spoke in broken Spanish, and then I got better. After a few months, I spoke fluent Spanish.

My nickname was Panama. I never knew why I was given that nickname. During the game, some guy would say, "Hey, Panama, get me cigarettes," or "Hey, Panama, get me some coffee," or anything else they wanted. I would run to the local deli and pick up coffee, sandwiches, and cigarettes. Upon my return, one of the men would give me a dollar. That was how I existed for many months. I still got an adrenaline rush just from watching the guys place their bets.

I remember one night when I finally had a big win. To celebrate, I walked into Tony's bar. I was feeling very good about myself, so I started buying drinks for everyone in the bar. There were about sixty people in the dark bar, including the dancers. On the jukebox, Donna Summers was singing "Love to Love You, Baby." I ordered another round for the entire bar. Looking around at all the patrons, I thought they looked pretty happy. In my mind, I imagined that everyone would soon realize that I was the big shot. So, how about the third round of drinks? However, I needed to relieve myself and excused myself to go to the restroom.

While I was at the urinal, a drunk staggered in. Without looking at me he said, "Hey, some asshole is out there buying free drinks for the whole bar. You better get out there and get one before he leaves."

I just looked at him and said, "Thanks, will do." This poor drunk did not even realize that he was talking to that "asshole."

That is one of my best examples of what happened time and time again in my effort to be seen as a bigshot. What strikes me about that example is that there may have been an eviction notice on the door of my apartment that same night. I certainly owed money to people all over the neighborhood. I probably even had holes in my shoes while I was buying other people drinks. Any rational person would've wondered to himself, "Why not pay off at least some of your debts, or pay your rent so you won't be homeless again?"

However, the big shot syndrome was part of my gambler mentality. I've heard people actually say "I knew I was destroying myself, but the table in the casino was the only place I felt comfortable." My gambling addiction also provided a sense that my schemes would pay off. Inevitably, for me, that fantasy would always turn into a nightmare.

I did try to connect with family again. They did not know about my gambling problem or that I had been evicted again. They did not know that I had been unemployed for more than a year. A new year was starting, and I was getting closer to finding a new life.

THE INVISIBLE ENEMY

It was the start of 1981. I found a place to sleep for the night. It was a rooftop. I told myself it was only for one night. The weather was cold but thankfully not snowing. I began talking to God like a man in a trap or a prison. There were no locked doors around me, but I felt like I was in a prison of my mind. I was imprisoned by my addiction and by the choices I had made in life.

I prayed, "God, please get me out here." I was praying that God would give me the key to the prison gates. Ultimately, he would hear my prayers. I would find the key to my prison. Nothing happens overnight. So, I went back to the social club again and hoped someone needed coffee.

I finally had a good day as a gofer. I must have made about ten trips to the deli, and I had at least $10 in my pocket. I walked over to the dice table and I bet five dollars. The dice game was set up on a large pool table. It was the same group of men I saw every night. I picked up the dice and I rolled, and I hit a *winner.* Something came over me then. I was angry and tired, and I was fed up with living like a dog. So I went all the way. I decided to press all my bets.

I'd never done this before. Pressing your bets means that you don't take your money off the table, but instead, you bet it all on the next roll of the dice. So I rolled again and I kept rolling. And every time, I hit seven or eleven. I hit a winner each time.

I kept rolling the dice, and I kept winning. I was screaming at the other men at the table because even a wimp can become a brave man with a pair of dice in his hand.

"Come on, you son of a bitch! Put the fucking money on the table! Where are your balls? Come on, fucking sissy, put it on the table, you got the fucking money?" I was enraged. They could see the veins in my neck as I yelled at each man.

The other men are puzzled, trying to figure out where the hell I had gotten any money from in the first place. They knew I was always flat broke. Now, I'm betting a thousand dollars on the table. Slowly, they remembered giving me dollars to get coffee. I could see the expression on their faces. They are thinking we gave this kid money; *Shit.*

I started calling out Country Sausage and Mafioso by name. Another Italian gangster named "Jimmy Jacks" became very pissed off at my insults. Everyone said that he was the real owner of the club. He reached into his wallet and pulled out a roll of hundred-dollar bills. He was determined to bet against me until he broke me. This unleashed the floodgate for all of the whales to place their bets, too, each one of them betting against me. I'm rolling the dice with twenty or twenty-five men standing around the table.

But every time I pick up the dice, I hit a winner. Remember that I was always a "right bettor," meaning that I always bet with the dice. Previously, I always ended up broke; but this night was different. This was the night I had been waiting for. I was the only "right bettor" left in the club. These guys, these "wrong bettors," believed that sooner or later I just had to lose. Yet, I continued to roll the dice. My number came up eight, and then I hit boxcars, a pair of fours. WOW! I WON! I WON!

And finally, I bet it all. I rolled the dice and looked to see that I had rolled a four: one dice on a one, and one dice on a three. We called the number four "Little Joe" because it is a difficult number to make. The other gamblers began to smile again. They believed that I was done.

Then, I had hit a four, I had hit Little Joe!!!

The moans of twenty-five men filled the room. I've never heard anything like it since. The game was over, and I had won. I "broke" the game. After long last, I was a winner.

I had won so much money that even after stuffing rolls into my front and back pockets, I still had to shove bills into my socks. I had money everywhere. I thought *I won't need to sleep on the subway anymore.* I turned and walked out of the club, euphoric with adrenaline. Winning was like the most powerful cocaine high. It was beyond any drug or orgasm I had ever had. I felt like I had broken the game wide open. I could hear the men mumbling as I walked out, they were pissed, and I was on a high.

Before I had made up my mind about where to go, I stopped to buy a cup of coffee. Now, it was three AM in the morning, and my pockets were holding thousands of dollars. Three men approached me.

The one behind me hit me over the head with a lead pipe and knocked me to the ground. The second guy smashed my head with a brick, and blood poured from my head. While I lay bleeding, the third guy rifled through my pockets. A hot minute later, they were gone, leaving me in the street in front of Joe & Mary's restaurant.

My mind spun with blood loss and disappointment. *This can't be happening—I'm supposed to be a winner tonight.* A passerby stopped to get me up on my feet. It occurred to me that this guy may have been with the crooks who robbed me. I'm still not sure. Yet, he helped me up and handed me something to staunch the cuts on my head, and then he walked with me the few blocks to Wyckoff Hospital. As soon as I entered the emergency room, the nurses rushed to stop my bleeding. They stitched my wound and bandaged me, then gave me some pills and sent me back out the door. The pills were antibiotics and painkillers. I took a few pills, but I had not eaten. So, I took pills on an empty stomach. I felt really dizzy, so I got on the subway and began my long nightly ride back and forth on the F train.

After sleeping for eight or nine hours, I was hungry. I put my hands in my pockets and there was no money—I almost forgot what happened last night. My head hurt. I touched the bandages. I saw blood, bandages were still wet. I checked in my jacket pocket—still no money. So I went out on the streets and panhandled so I could get my breakfast.

While I was standing there trying to get some loose change from any passerby, I was not thinking about the fact that I was mugged or about the fact that my head was broken open in three places, or about the blood still seeping through the bandages on my head. I was thinking about the dice game. I was reliving how I broke the game on Little Joe. Even today, I remember the look on the faces of the men when I hit those two deuces. I thought *the looks on their faces was worth all my cold nights on the subway, all those empty nights without a meal.*

I also remembered that rush of adrenaline, and I wanted to have that feeling one more time. I finally panhandled for two dollars and bought some coffee and a bagel. As I drank my coffee, I scratched my leg and was shocked to find something. "Oh my God!" I had a roll of money in my sock that the muggers hadn't found. There was almost $1,000.

I sat there with my heart pounding. I am thinking what should I do with the money? So, I returned to the underground casino on Knickerbocker and Jefferson. I knocked on the door. I wonder if they would let me in. They all knew that I was robbed last night, and was most likely broke again.

I looked like a mess. They could see that blood was seeping through the bandages on my head. But I looked at the men and smiled, saying, "I will break this goddamn game again, you sons of bitches, and this time I'll have a cab waiting outside."

The men looked at each other. They were talking with their eyes, saying to each other, "This guy is really sick." No one in their right mind would come back to this place after what had happened to him. I had been here losing every week for years, ultimately just being the guy who runs out for coffee and cigarettes. And after one lucky night, I'm almost killed. The men must have been thinking, "Why didn't we just put a bullet in his head?" They undoubtedly knew the guys who robbed me. Most of the time, when that much money was stolen, the thieves kill the guy. Instead, they just knocked me out, took the money, and left me bleeding in the streets. Any rational person would have run for their life, and yet, here I was, back again.

Why didn't they kill me? Maybe they knew about my brothers and knew that Gary and Richard would find out and come looking for them.

But, you know, business is business, so the dice game started. Two hours later, I was broke. I went back to my corner, waiting to see if anybody needed coffee or cigarettes. When the game was done, I went to find my brother Gary. I was confused. I was mad as hell and yet did not want to put my troubles on his shoulder. But, I told him what happened the night before.

Gary reacted instantly when I told him what happened. He took a large knife from the kitchen, put it under his jacket, and told me to wait for him near the subway.

"I know who did this to you," he said. "I'm going back to the club. Stay here and do not follow me."

I didn't listen. I waited a few minutes, and then I followed him. I clearly understood that Gary was going back to the club to kill Jimmy Jack who he was convinced was behind the setup. As Gary approached Knickerbocker Ave, he turned and spotted me across the street. He now knew that I had followed him. He changed course, walked back in my direction, and I could see he was annoyed.

"I wanted you to wait by the subway," he fumed. "I'm going to do it, and I'll do it quickly, and then I'll meet you later."

I told him, "I don't want this. I know what you're going to do, but it's going to be on *me*. I'll have to live with it. You might end up in jail, and that's no good, so I say no, don't do this."

Gary seemed even more annoyed. He warned me, "Mike, we have to send a message. These people are going to talk about this, and talk about you, talk about me… We have to send a message."

"They can talk all they want," I told him. "They can call me a punk and I don't care. I'm telling you, Gary, I don't want this for you. Let's go back."

Abruptly, he turned and headed back with me to the house. I do not doubt that if I hadn't followed him that evening, somebody would've been dead the next morning. Brooklyn was a very rough place to live.

The next morning, I threw away the bottle of pills the doctor had given me for my head injury. I did not understand why I need to finish the antibiotics. I think now that I should've taken those pills because they would have prevented infections. Thirty-seven years later, I still get headaches. My brother went back home to his wife Ronnie, and I jumped over the turnstile in the subway. So, I took the A Train back to Manhattan.

I returned to the library on 42nd Street and Fifth Avenue. I spent yet another day hiding among the bookshelves. I found more books to read, more warm corners to hide in. Even then, I was still thinking about the dice game and how it felt to win, to pick up the money and put it in my pocket. I could feel the hunger for another winning streak. I did wonder if I would ever win again.

However, that last night at the club was turning out to be a wake-up call. I was a loser, even on a winning night. I really didn't understand the power of denial and was not yet ready to accept what I later would call "the self-sabotage trap." I was spending more and more time in the library, and finding some interesting books. My mind was starting to change. I realized that I was not only in a trap, I was the architect.

I turned up at the 42nd Street library almost every single day. I would find a spot where I would not be seen or bothered, and I would crawl into a book for hours. Someone once said that "Reading a book allows a person to travel a thousand miles without moving an inch."

During that time, I read any and everything I could get my hands on. I read about politics and business. Once, I found a row of twenty-six small books in a line on the bookshelf. The title of the series was *The Warren Commission Report on the Assassination of Pres. John F. Kennedy.* I reached up, pulled out Volume 1, and began reading. Then, I read Volume 2 and Volume 3 and Volume 4 and— I read all twenty-six volumes over the next two days. I learned a lot about President Kennedy. The report cemented my opinion of him as a good, decent man, even though some people thought he was too young and something of a playboy. I disagree. I found him to be a truly amazing individual.

I also found books on self-help and motivation. These books would change my life. These were people who believed in the power of positive thinking, and the power of motivation. I found books by Les Brown, Tom Hopkins, Og Mandino, and Tony Robbins. I started thinking about my future for the first time in my life. I started to feel that the time had come for me to decide about my future. Was my destiny just to spend my days running from one casino or social club to the next, and then to the next racetrack? Why was I wasting my life on the streets, just trying to scrape up enough money to buy breakfast each day? It did not make much sense.

The time for me to make a change was very near. Yet, I had no idea how or in what way that change would take place. I was still in the grip of my gambling addiction, and addiction is a progressive illness that cannot be cured. Some people afflicted with this illness can never break free. I saw people all around me struggling with addiction to alcohol, drugs, sex, food, relationships, and, yes, gambling.

In most cases, I did not see these people ever experience a positive outcome. For some, the outcome was prison, insanity, or death. But, addiction is an illness that can be arrested, and I started questioning my part in the problem. I had to confront my complicity in my demise, that I was the mastermind of my life of self-sabotage

I was also in denial, and I struggled with low self-esteem and envy. I would look at the next person who was doing well in life and resent them for it. I wondered why I had not had better opportunities like that person. I spent my days stewing in jealousy. So, the journey to reclaim my destiny would be a challenge.

However, as I read more books, I understood the meaning of the words, "When one is truly ready for a thing, it appears." Or, as a friend once said to me, "Act as if." These words mean that before I could ever become a successful businessman, I needed to talk like a businessman, walk like a businessman, and look like a businessman. If a person wanted to be the President of the United States of America, that person would need to think like a president, sound like a president, and act like a president.

What I wanted to be was a person again. I wanted to feel like a human being again and I wanted a place to live: a place where I could lay my head down and get a good night's sleep in my own bed. I wanted to join the civilized world again. I wanted to escape from the underworld I now inhabited. This underworld only consisted of nights in the subway and cold food. How could I change my situation?

I turned up one afternoon at the men's shelter that has a soup kitchen on East 3rd Street, in the Bowery, lower Manhattan. This stretch was New York City's Skid Row. The place had a dark, dreary feeling. A long line of men waited outside the main entrance. They were all down on their luck. Some wore not much more than rags. I was not much better off myself, since sleeping on the subways for the last months without showering or brushing my teeth, or combing my hair.

As I mingled with the men sitting there, some drinking from a bottle of wine, some trying to bum a cigarette, others waiting for the soup kitchen to open, I realize that many of these men were once attorneys, bankers, doctors, professors, real estate brokers. Yet they were all there, having somehow fallen down on their luck, and I was there with them.

After a few minutes of standing in line and contemplating what to do, I felt a deeper emotion. It was as if a voice said to me, "Get off this line right now, Mike, or you'll be here for the rest of your life." I sensed that if I started down this path of standing in line for each meal, it would never end. I was beginning to understand compulsive behavior, and addiction. Since I was a master at playing games, I would learn how to play this game too. For a moment I was fearful that I would really waste my future. Against my judgment and my empty stomach, I stepped off the line and walked away.

I was starting to imagine that there must be more to life than my everyday cycle of winning and losing, mostly losing. I was also beginning to see that my way of rationalizing poor choices was leaving me nowhere. The life of a gambler is a no-win situation. I was beginning to reflect deep into my soul. I was starting to realize that if I wanted to change my circumstances, it was time to "Act as if" I would experience one more important lesson, and that lesson also involved what happens to my older brothers.

CASUALTIES OF LIFE

By the end of 1981, all three of my older brothers were in prison again. I visited Riker's Island almost every month and I wrote letters constantly. I was thinking that I should become a lawyer. As some of my brothers got older, they began to change their ways. They wanted freedom. Gary was the first to see the light. When we had the opportunity to talk about it later, he told me that after he finished his last five-year term, he knew that he never wanted to go back to prison again. I guessed that something had happened to him in prison.

People started getting sick in New York City. We did not understand the cause, it was a virus. We would later call that virus "AIDS." It would kill some of my family members, as well as millions of people in the years ahead. One day, I walked into a bar, and on the television was a wedding, a big wedding. Prince Charles had married Lady Diana. My favorite movie that year was called "Arthur" The story of a millionaire who was a drunk. I also loved the movie "Chariots of Fire". I also started to hear about a new drug on the street, they called it "Crack."

Gary got out of jail, and he did keep his word about staying out of prison. Unfortunately, by age 32, he was dead.

Of all my brothers, Gary was the one I admired the most. Gary had always had a lot of class and charisma. He had style, humor, confidence, and he was a ladies' man. He often was living with two or three women at the same time, though each lady might not have known it. One year, two of his ladies, Rosemary and Francis, got pregnant at the same time. They both named their sons Gary Williams, Jr. My brother couldn't say a word because he didn't want the two women to know about each other.

Gary was very different from Richard. Richard was more emotional, a hothead, unforgiving. Anyone who double-crossed Richard would end up hurt. By contrast, Gary was a businessman. I heard a rumor that he was once paid to "find a drug dealer" and collect money from the guy. That drug dealer was never seen again.

I do not know if this story was true because I was not a witness. However, that would explain why I was almost killed at the Tiptop Lounge when the guy with the shotgun approached me. It was clear that the guy was there to settle a score.

Yes, Gary was strictly business, and everybody in the neighborhood knew that about him.

Once his reputation as "Gary Dangerous" started to spread in Brooklyn, he rarely had any disputes with anyone. Everyone knew he was a guy to take seriously. They also knew that I was his little brother. I soon had a reputation as his brother. It started with a few drunks were sitting on a corner. Gary and I walked by, and the first drunk said, "That's Dangerous!" Then he saw me and added, "and dangerous little brother." He meant to say that I was the little brother of Gary Dangerous, but the second drunk only heard the last part and started telling everyone in the neighborhood that I was "a dangerous little brother".

I can imagine him a few months later, I would walk by them alone, and the drunks were telling people I was a serial killer. That's what happens when you get a few drunks on a corner with nothing to do but talk.

I was with Gary almost to the end. The night before he died, I was with him in Brooklyn. Then I went back to Staten Island to meet my lady Sally, who later became my wife. While I was with her, I got a phone call that my brother Gary was dead. I had not even known that he used intravenous drugs, and I certainly never imagined that drugs would be what killed him after everything he went through on the streets.

To my surprise, he left enough money in his bank account to pay for his funeral. I purchased a gravesite for him in Rosedale Cemetery in New Jersey. I had never bought a grave before, so I paid little attention to the fact that the gravesite that I purchased was able to hold three caskets. I laid Gary to rest there, and I purchased a tombstone with his name on it. This was the final act of my love for my older brother.

Frank followed Gary's lead and did not go back to prison. However, Frank had died at age 37. I had never gotten along well with Frank because we had lived together in the group home. When I got into fights with the other boys, he rooted against me. We had a difficult time growing up. Still, I cared for him as my brother.

Frank spent the last two years of his life as a homeless man and also died from drug abuse. We had a funeral for Frank and I put his casket in the same grave as Gary. There was still a space for one more casket.

However, before Richard, Gary, or Frank, there was the first born. Harold was the oldest of the 12 children. Harold had a hard life too and died at the young age of 26 because of drugs and alcohol. He was the apple of my mother's eye. Yet, her first marriage ended badly. Harold lived with his father at first, then on his own for some years. Like me, he was an artist. Always a sharp dresser, and I am sure a ladies' man. He lived a fast and short life. Consumed by drugs and drink. He left behind a wife, Sharon, a son, Harold, and a daughter, Glynis.

Richard, on the other hand, was the one always in trouble. It seemed that he was angry at the world and lived in the fast lane. I saw a message in his eyes, "I want my revenge." Richard was involved in everything from street gangs, crime, and the drug business. It was not unusual to find Richard on a warm summer night driving a stolen car with a gun in his belt buckle and a pretty girl on his arm. He and his girlfriend Val were right out of the movie *Bonnie and Clyde.*

Sooner or later I would get another letter from Riker's Island. Like I talked about earlier, I visited Richard in places like Attica, Dannemora, and Comstock. His last court date, when he was convicted of first-degree murder, was in early 1992. That experience haunts me at times.

Richard was accused of killing a drug dealer on a street in Harlem in broad daylight. I talked with him about this case many times. He would look me in my eyes and say, "Mike, I swear on mama's grave, I did not kill that man." His words sounded sincere to me.

His trial was held on a cold February morning. I arrived at 100 Centre Street wearing a dark blue suit with a matching navy tie. I carried my briefcase and a newspaper. I was anxious, and I hesitated before I approached his public defender. Mr. Blackstone also appeared very nervous. He seemed concerned that if he lost this case, his safety would be at risk. When he spoke to me, I noticed how his hand would tremble. I expected this trial to go on for a few days, but to my surprise, it was over in about three hours. The jury returned a quick verdict of guilty, convicting Richard of murder in the first degree.

I remember that the assistant district attorney, Mr. Donahue, explained to the judge that the defendant Richard Williams was a career criminal. He wanted Richard sentenced to prison for the rest of his natural life and recommended life without parole, based on Richard's criminal background. The prosecutor pointed out that Richard Williams had been arrested over twenty-two times before the age of twenty-four and that some of the crimes were felony convictions. He charged that Richard Williams was a three-time loser.

As the assistant district attorney spoke to the judge, I waited for the defense attorney to interrupt, but he never said a word. My brother would later charge him with ineffective counsel.

I felt self-conscious sitting there in the courtroom. I imagined that people knew I was the accused's younger brother. Even though I was dressed in a very nice suit and tie with a briefcase, I imagined that people were thinking, *He's probably just like his brother, he's probably a thief or drug dealer, too.* I wanted to get up and walk out of the courtroom.

The judge started to speak, and his words were much harsher than the prosecutor. "You have been convicted of murder in the first degree and you are convicted of a crime which I can only describe as a 'narcotics assassination.'"

Those words would ring in my ears for years. Could my brother have really done this?

As Richard was led away by the guard, he turned to look at me. His hands were cuffed and his feet were shackled. With my eyes, I tried to tell him that I would always be there for him. I somehow managed to keep that promise. For better or for worse, he was my oldest brother now.

For the next twenty-five years, I wrote letters and I visited him regularly, even though every few years they moved him from one penitentiary to the next. They were concerned that if he was in one place for too long, he would organize groups of men. Richard did admit to me that in prison, he did what he had to do to survive. So, in the beginning, he was involved with some rough groups.

However, over time, he changed. Richard found religion and converted to Islam. I noticed a different person on my visits to the prisons. At first, I was cautious. I was not sure this conversion was not just another gimmick. I later learned the change was real.

During my visits, I sat and talked to Richard for hours. I wanted to know why he had so much trouble in his life. He said it was because of society, the system, and racism. I would think about the movie *The Shawshank Redemption.* I'm not sure my brother realized how much he reminded me of the character Red. In the movie, there's a scene where Red, played by Morgan Freeman, goes before the parole board. He tells them that he wishes he could go back and talk to his younger self, who was so stupid and naïve. However, he says, "It's too late. That young man is long gone, and all you have now is this old man sitting here."

One day in the visiting room at Clinton Correctional Facility, I told Richard that I had decided to become a lawyer. Honestly, I figured that between my brothers and their friends, I would have a lot of clients. Richard told me he believed that I would be a great lawyer and he hoped I could help him with his case.

In 2018, after serving twenty-five years, Richard told me that he was being considered for parole. If it was granted, he would be on parole for the rest of his life. I was surprised to hear that he was even being considered. I remembered the assistant DA who wanted Richard sentenced to life without parole, talking about the fact that Richard was a career criminal and should never walk the streets again.

My brother wanted to go before the board and insist on his innocence. I told him it was too late for that, and that he had already served the time for that crime. I remembered another movie, *The Count of Monte Crisco.* Abbé Faria, played by Richard Harris, tells Edmond Dantès upon escape to not commit the crime for which he had just served the sentence.

I told my brother, "You have to pick your battles. This is a battle that you already lost." I told him that he needed to go before the board and talk about his future. I advised him to tell the board how much he regretted what happened to the families, and how much he regretted what he had done with his younger years. Finally, I told him, tell the board what you want to do with the rest of your life.

I had given my brother advice in the past and it had never done much good before. So, I was shocked when he sent me a letter that summer telling me that he would be released from prison in October.

Of all his time in jails, Richard had cumulatively spent more than forty years of his life behind bars. Now, he was ready to walk out as a free man. I thought about *The Shawshank Redemption* again, but this time I thought about the character Brooks. Brooks was an older man who had spent the majority of his life behind bars. When Brooks is finally released into the strange outside world, all he wants is to return to the prison, the world he is familiar with. I was likewise concerned about Richard. Namely, my brother was an important man on the inside. He had respect and power among the inmates. Now he was going to walk out the door and become just another guy on the street.

During our last visit before he was released, I looked into my brother's eyes, the eyes of an older man now, and I could feel his concern. I saw a man who was not sure that he was ready to leave prison.

Richard had been incarcerated almost nonstop since he was seventeen years old. He did not need to think about where he would lay his head at night to sleep, a problem that I often faced as a gambler while living on the streets. While I slept in old abandoned buildings, Richard always had a bed. He had three meals a day. Yet, he would gladly trade places with me and I would not under any conditions want to trade places with him. Now the question was whether he could adjust to living as a free man. Many of his friends were convinced he would be back in prison in no time.

But when Richard walked out of the door of Queensboro Correctional Facility on October 1, 2018, he dropped to his knees and kissed the ground. I vividly remember the scene. At nine o'clock in the morning, I stood outside the prison. I heard a buzzing and a clicking sound, then the metal door opened. A group of men walked out onto the sidewalk. In the crowd, I saw the face of my brother.

He first looked up at the sky. Then he looked around and saw where I was calmly leaning against a car. I was holding a brand new, empty gray suitcase. This time the suitcase wasn't for me to fill with cash but was to help my brother carry his belongings.

We tossed the contents of his duffel bag into the suitcase as we walked towards the subway. He was a free man now, breathing the free air.

I asked him, "What do you want for breakfast?" I had made a point not to eat anything that morning so that we could have a good meal together.

Richard looked around and spotted a hot dog vendor on the corner. He said, "Man, I want me a hotdog!"

"Are you crazy?" I asked. "It's 9 a.m.! We need to get ourselves pancakes, eggs, coffee, or something!"

"Mike, I'm telling you, man, I want me a hotdog." My brother had been a free man for three minutes and he was making bad decisions already.

What the hell, I thought, let's go to the hot dog vendor. I was getting irritated, but Richard approached the hotdog vendor with a big smile on his face and ordered a hotdog with ketchup.

"Are you out of your mind?" He looked at me and smiled. I told him, "Nobody eats a hotdog with ketchup! You mean you want a hotdog with mustard, right?"

Richard looked at me like I didn't know what I was talking about and said, "I've been dreaming about a hotdog with ketchup for a long time."

I just had to laugh. After I paid the vendor for the hotdog, we walked to the subway that would bring us to his parole officer. We waited for a few minutes and then saw a sign saying that the train was delayed. Richard was now getting agitated and impatient.

I looked at him strangely. "You just spent twenty-five years in prison but can't wait ten minutes for the subway?"

Richard smiled, but he kept scratching his pants leg. I had given him some money that he had put in his pocket. I remembered my mother saying, "That money just burns a hole in his pocket." He suggested that we catch a cab instead.

I shook my head. I said, "You've only been free for seven minutes, and let me tell you the mistakes you've already made. First, you ordered a hotdog for breakfast—then you ordered it *with ketchup*.

Now you want to take a taxicab to your parole officer just because I gave you a hundred dollars. Do you realize how expensive a yellow cab in New York City is?"

Richard thought about this and he started laughing again. I said we should just wait for the train, and he said okay, but then a cab passed us. Like a little kid in a candy store, he yelled "Taxi!" and waved it down. I imagine this was probably something he saw in a movie while in prison. As we drove in the cab, he looked out the window at the world, just grinning. He could feel the wind was on his face. For him, it was a very strange feeling.

After we visited the parole officer, we had one more stop to make. We picked up a mobile phone for him at the convenience store. Oddly, he seemed to know how to use a cell phone quite well.

I was going to drop him off at the men's shelter near Bellevue Hospital. At the shelter, he was guaranteed a place to sleep that night. Most importantly, this shelter offered a program to assist with the re-entry process. On our way there, he said, "Maybe I can check in later. I want to go see some friends." He noticed my immediate reaction. I said, "Let's stick to the plan." After a few minutes, Richard agreed that he could always make the trip to see his friends in Harlem the next day.

As he walked into the shelter, carrying his new suitcase, he stopped and turned to look at me, and I again saw concern in his eyes. I reassured him, "Don't worry, big brother, it will all work out alright. You're a free man now, you're free at last." Richard tried to smile back at me, and then he went in.

I was sure he would figure things out, and I trusted that the shelter would give him a bed and would help with meals. Plus he had some family that would help him, too. After what he had been through, I was sure he could make it.

Later that night, Richard called me with the prepaid phone to let me know he was all checked in. We did not talk long. He ended the call by saying, "Mike, I'm looking out the window and for the first time in my life that I can remember, I don't see any bars on the windows. Good night, little brother. I love you."

For now, his last term in prison was his turning point. I watched him find his way over the next few months. He was not wasting time. First, he found a job and then found Susan, who became his wife. I think that his last prison term was the turning point.

As for me, my turning point had arrived on a cold October afternoon in 1981. I did not know then that my life would change in the time it takes to finish a cup of coffee, and yet it did. I did not know that I would finally find the way out of my own prison.

CHAPTER 3

"He who saves the life of one saves the world entire."

Talmud

HOT COFFEE AND DIVINE INTERVENTION

It was 1982, and there was a dark cloud over New York City. The crack cocaine problem was getting out of control. I saw an article in a newspaper about a big drug bust, some guy named John Delorean took a gamble to save his company. There was another story about a serial killer arrested in Atlanta, a man named Wayne Williams.

My favorite movie that year was "Gandhi" I loved movies that were 3 hours long. The longer the movie the better. I also managed to see a movie called " The Verdict" I still dreamed that one day I would go to law school. I spend that night sleeping on the F train.

That next day started like most other days. I had spent the night sleeping in on the train and I woke up cold, tired, and hungry. I was panhandling inside the Union Square subway station, trying to scrape up a few dollars for breakfast. There, a stranger offered to buy me a cup of coffee.

This man looked to be about thirty years old. Carrying his jacket over his arm, he was wearing a sweater and dark pants. He was a black man with a type of face that I found not too threatening; with his short Afro haircut, he could have easily been mistaken for my brother Harold. I think he even reminded me of my brother who died at age 26. So, I approached him while he waited for the train.

"Excuse me, sir, can I trouble you for a quarter? I really need to get something to eat."

He looked at me and asked, "What on earth can you buy to eat with a quarter?"

"Not much, but if I get another quarter from someone else, I could get myself a coffee. I haven't had a full meal in a day and a half."

This was the truth. Sometimes I would say I hadn't had a meal in three days when in fact it had only been one, but on this day it was true that I hadn't eaten in early two days. The man looked down for a second, and then he looked over my shoulder at a nearby coffee shop.

"I tell you what," he said. "I'll buy you a cup of coffee at that coffee shop right there."

"Okay! Let's go!" I figured that this fella thought I was a drunk or a junkie, and thought it was safer to buy me coffee instead of giving me any money. That was fine with me since I was truly hungry.

Where we sat was not so much a coffee shop as a coffee stand, just a long counter with a clerk in a white cap standing on the other side. On the customer side were small metal stools to sit on. In front was a row of doughnuts and corn muffins. A sign advertised that a cup of coffee and a sandwich was $1.50. A baseball game was playing on the clerk's radio.

We sat down. I tried to look straight ahead, well aware of the noise my stomach was making. I could smell chicken and hotdogs, and getting close to that food increased my hunger. The stranger sitting next to me noticed me staring at the fried chicken.

"That fried chicken looks really good, doesn't it?" he asked me. He turned to the clerk and ordered us each a chicken sandwich and a cup of coffee. I added some milk and sugar to my coffee and tried not to scarf down my chicken sandwich too fast. It was the best damn sandwich I've ever eaten. I was proud of myself for not eating the bones.

The man started to talk to me. "Do you think it is time to change your way of life? How long will you continue to lie to yourself?" I don't remember every word of what he said, but what he did next changed my whole perspective on life.

He moved the jacket from his arm to take his money out of his pocket to pay the clerk. I noticed he had a bandage on his arm. At first, I paid no attention to it. When he placed a five-dollar bill on the counter to pay for the sandwich and the coffee, I noticed that the bill had a few drops of blood on it. To be polite to the stranger who had just brought me breakfast, I asked, "I see you have a bandage on your arm. Did you hurt yourself?"

"Oh no, little brother. I just sold five dollars' worth of blood at the blood bank," he said as he collected his change from the clerk.

He stood up. His final words to me were, "Whatever you do, you have to start being true to yourself, little brother." Then the stranger walked away. He had called me little brother twice, and he was about the age my brother Harold would have been if he had still been alive.

I sat for a while staring at my empty cup of coffee and I had an epiphany. My hand began to tremble. I realized that this stranger had just sold his blood at a blood bank, which meant he was probably not doing all that well himself. But, he chose to use that money to feed me, a perfect stranger. I did not feel worthy. I felt like I should have told him the truth. I am a gambling junkie. This moment changed my life.

I wondered, *Could I sell my own blood at a blood bank and then use the money to feed a stranger?* I knew that I did not have it in my heart to do that for anyone. The fact is, if I had any money at all, I would use it to make a bet. I sat a little longer trying to understand how someone could do that.

The moment became spiritual. I felt myself changing. I felt for the first time that I could face my fears. I felt for the first time I needed to stop lying to myself.

I had to stop lying to other people, too. I kept telling people I was having trouble finding a job when I wasn't even looking for work. I kept telling people I was struggling because I was encountering racism at every turn, even though the folks that were trying to help me were both white and black. At that moment, I knew that all of my lies had to stop. At that moment, I saw the old me dying and a new person being born. It was the birth of a new freedom.

I walked away from the coffee stand and I knew there was no turning back. I began walking into office buildings looking for a job. I told people that I would take any available job. It was still early in the afternoon. I was walking door to door looking for work.

When I walked into the office building on 41st Street and Fifth Avenue, I hesitated before going upstairs. The location was quite familiar because the public library was right across the street. The company was called Fargo Overland Security, and I felt that there was a chance that they may be looking for a security guard.

I was surprised to see two security guards sitting at the front desk in the lobby since it was a Saturday. Both guards were wearing blue uniforms and labels that said "Fargo Overland Security." One of them was reading a newspaper. When I opened the door, they gave me a strange look. They could likely tell that I was a guy with problems. My clothes were disheveled, and they may have noticed the smell as I had not had a bath in several months. It didn't take a genius to figure out that I was homeless.

But I spoke quickly. "Can you tell me if any companies in this building have any jobs available?" One of them told me I could go to the third floor and see the security guard at the front desk, because they may have some jobs open for security guards.

I went upstairs and decided to think more positively as I approached the next two guards at the front desk. I said, "Good morning, I understand you might be looking for security guards. I hope I can sign up for some work."

The guards seemed like they were trying to hold their noses a little bit, and one guard told me they didn't have any openings—maybe I should come back next week. The other guard interrupted. "I think there is a job open at Hunts Point in the Bronx."

Being from the South Bronx, I knew exactly where Hunts Point was and I told them so. The first security guard said, "Here, take this uniform inside the bathroom and try it on. We may send you to work today."

The uniform didn't fit well. The pants were too short and the jacket was too long. But I was not going to take any chance, so I made it work. I used my teeth to tear out the seam in the pants, and I made them longer. I turned the sleeves on the jacket inward and made the jacket shorter. I stepped outside the bathroom and I saluted the two guards.

Both security guards started laughing and they told me I looked like a clown. But they needed somebody to take that job in Hunts Point, so they went ahead and sent me to work. I jumped over the turnstile to take the train up to the Bronx.

The token booth clerk gave me a strange look—she didn't understand why a police officer was jumping the turnstile!

When I arrived at the assignment, I called in and confirmed I was there for the 4-to-12 shift. I then said a prayer that the midnight guy would not show up so that I would have a place to stay for the night. The midnight guy did not show up, and so I worked the afternoon and midnight shifts every day for the next three weeks. There was a coffee truck outside, and I convinced the guy to give me a sandwich and coffee until I got my first check. He did. I now believed that God was helping me help myself.

At the end of the first week, I had worked eighty-five hours. I worked one hundred and five hours the next week, and one hundred and nine hours the third week. The fourth week, the President of Fargo Overland Security called me into his office. He said, "Who the hell is this guy? I want to meet Michael Williams."

So, when I walked into President Michael Stern's office, he asked me why I worked so many hours. I replied, "Don't you wish you had a hundred more men like me?" He said, "If I had a hundred more men like you, I would be a mega-millionaire today."

We talked for a while and I told him a bit about my life. We seemed to connect, and I got the impression he was impressed. Finally, he looked up at the ceiling as if he was thinking about something very hard. Finally, he said, "I think I will do something a little different today. I want to promote you to a supervisor right now." I hesitated. I became a little anxious when he said that. I was happy to just have a job and to be getting a steady paycheck. No need to rock the boat. But, I became a bit inspired by his faith in me. We had just met.

I told him, "Mr. Stern, I really appreciate the promotion, but you have some men working here who have not had a promotion in years." Mr. Stern replied, "They haven't had a promotion in years because they never earned one." He decided, "I will make you the new supervisor of Division III. You'll have about forty-five security guards in your unit." He looked me up and down and added, "First, let's do something about that uniform."

He picked up the phone and called in the tailor. A man walked in with a measuring tape and I stood up while he measured me. In a few minutes, he returned with a brand-new uniform that fit me perfectly. When I walked out the door, I felt like a black Douglas MacArthur.

Honestly, I was in shock. All of a sudden, I had forty-five security guards under my command, including the two guys who had hired me only three weeks ago, who had teased me because they knew I was homeless. Now they watched me walk out of the president's office, wearing my new uniform with lieutenant bars. These guys were now in my unit and under my supervision. I would also have the assignment at Platt University- Women's Colgate Games. We provided the security detail.

However, one of the front desk officers threatened to quit when he learned that I had been promoted to a supervisor with only three weeks on the job. He was even more shocked when he learned that I was the supervisor of Division III. I completely understood. However, I saw him a week later when I reported to work.

I asked him, "Weren't you about to quit? What happened?"

He answered, "I was gonna' quit until my wife told me she would kill me if I came home without a job." I told him that I thought we would get along just fine as long as we both did what we were supposed to do.

I worked at Fargo Overland Security for nearly two years. During this time, I found myself having difficulty readjusting to the real world. I now had a furnished room and a key in my pocket, so I did not have to sleep in the subways anymore. Yet, when I went home at night, I would just lay in my bed and just stare at the ceiling. I would go to work the next day without any sleep. I couldn't sleep in my furnished room. The room was too quiet, and the bed was too clean.

So, I got up at 3 AM, put on my clothes, and got on the subway. On the train again, I was sound asleep in ten minutes. I needed the noise and the shaking of the train car to put me to sleep. I continued with this madness for a few weeks. I still went home, and I would lay in my bed for a couple of hours before realizing that I had to get some sleep before my 8 o'clock shift.

So, I would get on the train at about three in the morning, and I would fall asleep. There I would get five hours of sleep before arriving at the job for my 8-to-4 shift.

I finally told myself, "This is ridiculous." I said a prayer, asking God for help again. This was the first prayer I said since that night in that abandoned building on Myrtle Avenue when I had prayed, "Please God, get me out here." This time I prayed to be able to sleep in my own bed. Within a few minutes, it was like I had been hit in the head with a baseball bat. I was knocked out cold. My mother would say, "Think before you ask God for something"

I continued working hard at Fargo Security, and yet I had a sense it was just the start. I was now on my journey, a rendezvous with reality. I was offered a job to work security at the front door at Macy's in Herald Square. I was so proud to wear that maroon jacket and gray pants. Once again, I was back to working over a hundred hours a week. I worked for seven days, two shifts. I even worked a 24-hour shift at times.

I also started looking for a book that I had overheard someone talking about. The book was called *The Laws of Success*, written by Napoleon Hill. He had also written a book called *Think and Grow Rich.* I began to read his books every day and I became fascinated with his concepts. Hill wrote that whatever a person can conceive in their mind and believe in their heart, they can then achieve. I loved this type of thinking. It was a fit for my current state of mind. I knew it was time to face the enemy. I wanted to confront my demons of self-doubt, self-denial, self-sabotage, and procrastination.

Some quotes from those books held great meaning for me during those years. Hill said, "We are what we think." I began to learn about the "power of positive thinking." I began to perceive that a person needs to have a plan to move forward in life. To me, this meant that I needed to change myself and make clear my goals. I needed to confront my addiction first, and then, the lies needed to stop. The need to impress people must stop. It was time to be myself. So, I made a list of goals.

Napoleon Hill suggested that I read my list of goals every morning, repeating them so that they would reach my subconscious mind. I found this advice a bit strange, but I completed my list of what I wanted to change and my plans for the future. I started to read this list out loud to myself every morning, in a very low voice so that nobody else could hear me.

I was still struggling with my demons, even though I now slept in my own bed at night. Once in a while, I enjoyed an evening out with the other security guards. Most of them saw that there was something not quite right with me. I was still struggling with my gambling addiction.

Sometimes I would approach one of the other guards and say, "Hey man, let me borrow ten bucks." He would look at me strangely because it was Thursday and therefore payday. He'd say to me, "Man, just go cash your paycheck."

I'd insist, "I'll cash it later—hey man, just give me ten bucks right now." My security guard friend would not know that I had cashed my paycheck that morning and had already lost all my money at the OTB during the first three races.

So I made a phone call. I found help. I finally joined a self-help group that was able to help me address my problem of compulsive gambling. I met a lot of good people in that group, and I also talked to some professionals who gave me advice. I also read more books about confronting my addiction to gambling. The book that really had the most impact was called "Compulsion; Story of an Addicted Gambler."

One of the guys I met in the recovery group was named Dale. He was from a well-to-do Jewish family. However, he had gotten himself into deep trouble with gambling and had been arrested by his employer for stealing money. We met just before he ended up in jail and became good friends. During those months before his arrest, we often went to the clubs together to try to meet girls.

I was trying to clean up after a lifetime of gambling, but I couldn't solve all of my problems overnight. I was still having some problems with my finances. As a result, I couldn't pay my rent for my room and once again I was evicted.

I told Dale that I had lost my furnished room and was back on the streets again. He had just moved in with a young woman in New Jersey. However, Dale had a brilliant idea. His parents had gone to Florida for the summer and their apartment on the East Side of Manhattan was empty.

They owned a very expensive duplex apartment in a high-rise building on 33rd Street and Third Avenue. The unit had four bedrooms, three bathrooms, and a doorman. Dale gave me the keys and said I could stay until I earned a few more paychecks and could rent a furnished room again.

It was a generous offer in theory; however, Dale did not share this plan with his parents or his brother, who sometimes visited the apartment. Additionally, he did not tell any of the neighbors, or even the doorman, that a young African-American man would be residing there during the summer. This was about to turn into a different version of the movie *Guess Who's Coming to Dinner.* We could call it "Have You Met My Black Brother?"

So, on a warm June afternoon, I showed up with my suitcase and a big smile. I greeted the doorman and asked which elevator I should take to the twenty-fifth floor. I mentioned that I was a guest of Dale and showed the doorman that I had my own key.

The doorman gave me a strange look but he directed me to the elevator in the rear. The first few days of my stay were absolute bliss. I developed a habit of fixing myself a drink, vodka and orange juice, and sitting out on the terrace. From there, I waved to all of my new neighbors, a very big grin on my face.

My neighbors, in turn, returned my greetings with questioning looks. A few times, I imagined they even looked shocked to see me. I'm sure some of them considered calling the police. To add to the intrigue, one evening I invited a young lady from the Macy's cosmetics department to visit me there. She was from Brazil but she looked white. She had a beautiful body, blonde hair, and blue eyes. She looked like a fashion model, and I already had some fantasies in my mind about her. She took me up on my invitation and we sat out on the terrace, enjoying our drinks.

The next day, after I came home from work, I got undressed and I put on one of the robes in the closet that belonged to Dale's father. Then, I sat out on the terrace, drink in my hand, smoking a cigarette. I was feeling pretty good until I heard the doorbell ring. That was odd—I wasn't expecting any guests that evening.

I opened the door to see a man who had to be Dale's older brother. He had a puzzled look on his face. I asked the only thing I could: "May I help you?"

He replied, "Sure, You can tell me what the hell you're doing in my apartment!"

I explained that I was a good friend of Dale's and that he had given me the keys to the apartment so that I could stay there for a few days. Dale's brother's face was now red. He replied, "Well, I have a very big problem with that, and I'm sure my parents would also have a big problem! Dale has no goddamn right to give you the keys to this house without anyone's permission."

He then told me, "I would appreciate it if you would take your things and get the hell out of here right now."

I offered, "Are you sure you don't want to talk to Dale first?"

His face grew even redder and he replied: "I'll talk with him plenty later on! What I really need right now is for you to leave!"

I calmly thought, *So I am getting evicted again.* So what? At this point in my life, I couldn't get too angry about being back on the streets again. I had grown so accustomed to being evicted from one place after the next that it hardly even bothered me anymore. At least I had had a grand time for that one week. So, I packed up my suitcase and left.

I spent a few nights on the trains, and when I got my paycheck I checked into a room at the Benjamin Franklin Hotel located on 77th Street and Broadway. Ultimately, I would live at the Ben Franklin Hotel for almost two years. I would pay my rent weekly, I would continue to meet with my 12 step recovery groups, and I would continue to stay away from gambling. I was finally starting to learn that there is no such thing as something for nothing.

I was convinced that I was on the right path, even though I still felt strange waking up in the morning and repeating, out loud, all the items on my to-do list. It was better than reading my racing form. Unlike the days when my only obsession was gambling and making the big win, now I had other dreams, like someday opening my own business. I dreamed about different types of companies that I could start, and I still had a dream of going to law school and becoming an attorney.

Reading books revealed to me what I needed to do to change my life. As I read and reread the same books, they provided powerful examples for me.

From time to time my old demons returned to talk to me. I would hear the old tapes playing in my head. I could feel Atlantic City calling me back. Each time I felt that call, it was more seductive. Sometimes I saw advertisements for the casinos on the television, and I would feel that adrenaline rush again.

I can't deny that I missed it, and I was tempted to believe that maybe it would be different this time. I wanted to visit Atlantic City again. But I knew I had to stay on this new path. I needed to give myself a chance, even though I would always be a compulsive gambler and would continue to struggle with this illness. It was time to believe.

Ultimately, what I learned was that for the compulsive gambler, no-win would ever be big enough. My old way of life was a waste. I believed that if I applied my time and energies toward something more positive, the results would be quite different. So, I continued searching for the answers that could help me find a way forward. I finally started to meet the right people.

THE TEACHER APPEARS

I met a few people who could motivate me, but I was also fortunate to find a person who became a mentor. I was feeling better about myself since I'd gotten something of a grip on my gambling addiction, but everyday life still has many ups and downs. I had real struggles with money. I still had many debts to pay off. I still did not handle money well in general. I needed direction.

One of the key people to come into my life was a man named Ronald Davis. I've heard it said, "When the student is ready, the teacher will appear." Ron and I met at a time in my life when this student was finally ready. I knew him from my old neighborhood.

It was the end of 1983, and by some miracle, I had not made a bet or gambled in over a year. Ron was a big part of what had changed in my life. He was the first person to impress upon me that you are what you think. He had also grown up on the mean streets, but when I met him he worked in Manhattan's diamond district and was known as Ron the Jeweler.

He would be the first person to give me some lessons about sales and how to be a businessman. He also was the person who directed me towards the books by Napoleon Hill. He was one of the first to inspire me to leave security work and find a job in sales.

Ron was not much of a gambler, but he did have a problem with alcohol. To my deep sadness, he was eventually destroyed by the bottle. We lost contact after a few years, but it was clear that alcoholism had taken its toll. Yet, for those few years that I knew Ron, up until about 1991, he was one of the most important people in my life.

I seemed to meet the right people now. Kevin Jones was one of those individuals who changed the direction of my life. He was a co-worker and true friend, he influenced me to start a new career in sales and marketing. We both experienced some of the ups and downs in life. Yet, Kevin was a motivation force, and still a good friend to this very day.

Another good friend was Mickey, we belonged to the same 12 step recovery group. Mickey had joined the group about four years before I did, and he became a source of inspiration and a resource for knowledge. He was someone I could call on for advice when things got rough. I was l still looking for anything that could motivate me to move in a positive direction, and Mickey provided the kind of guidance I needed to maintain my forward focus.

I had slowly abandoned my delusions of winning a pot of gold. I had come to terms with the fact that there's no such thing as a quick fix. I had even started to manage my money a little better. For the first time in my life, I even saved enough money to buy a plane ticket, and I took a trip to Nassau in the Bahamas. I remember how nervous I was on my first flight. I almost went into shock when I saw the beach there. The water was incredible. I could stand in the water up to my chest and still see my feet. This was quite different from Coney Island, where the water is extremely dirty and sometimes contains waste, and visitors find themselves swimming with beer cans floating by.

The people in the Bahamas were also different. They said good morning and had warm smiles. There, I finally realized that by not gambling, I could become a winner. I returned from that trip ready to put my obsessive-compulsive behavior to work, turning a condition that had been a liability into an asset.

I began to dream. I began to expand my network, and reach out to more people. I was becoming a person again. Then, I wanted to be a motivational speaker, so I called group homes around the city and offered to talk with the boys. I visited group homes very much like the group home in Queens. In particular, I felt I needed to reach out to young black boys, and talk about the mistakes I had made, so they wouldn't have to spend their years living as I had.

I wanted to tell these young men not to fall for the trick of believing they can get something for nothing in life. It's true that some people get stuck and are stymied by poverty and racism, and have to just do the best they can. But some can do better, folks like me. I probably could've gotten off the street years earlier if I hadn't kept chasing the jackpot myth. Instead, I got scraps and almost paid with my life.

I am reminded of a poem I read in a book by Napoleon Hill

> I bargained with Life for a penny
> And life would pay no more
> However, I begged in the evenings
> As I counted my scant store.
>
> For life is a just employer,
> It gives you what you ask.
> Once you set the wages,
> You must bear the task.
>
> I worked for a menial hire,
> Only to learn, dismayed,
> That any wage I had asked of life,
> Life would have willingly paid.

I understood that it was up to me to decide on my price in life. I now began to embrace the principles of self-help and motivation, and I was starting to believe in myself. I put all my plans into writing. I wrote a one-year plan, a five-year plan, and a ten-year plan. I thought *I can decide the direction I'm sailing and I can decide what my goals are. I am the captain of my soul. And if I can believe it, then I can conceive it, and then one day, I can achieve it.*

However, I was reminded from time to time about my inner demons. They did not ever go away completely.

The demon that plagued me the most was my low self-esteem. I constantly had to build up my own confidence, time, and again. It seemed that no matter what my achievement was, I doubted myself every time. My battle for self-esteem and self-worth became a primary goal. I also had other battles as well with the demons of depression, anxiety, and stress. I sometimes had to fight the demons of envy and jealousy.

My fight to build self-esteem, and self-worth was constant work, but I was beginning to believe that anything I committed my mind to could become a reality. So, I began to dress like a successful person, I began to talk like a successful person, I began to walk like a successful person. I began to buy into the idea that I could be successful.

I think my self-esteem and sense of self-worth were beginning to heal. I also remember being told to "Act as if."

I also began to learn how to turn my energies around in a positive direction. I remember the first time I experienced this reversal. It was a warm, rainy June afternoon in 1985, shortly after I had started my new sales job with a company called Temp Positions, Inc. It was my first day in "the field" It was my first time "cold calling" a location, and I had just walked into the Chrysler building.

I was wearing my gray three-piece suit and a dark blue tie and carrying my briefcase and an umbrella. I was anxious because there was so much that I did not know about making sales calls. However, I was beginning to understand the power of my obsessive-compulsive behavior, and this was a chance to direct that behavior towards a positive goal.

By now I was aware of my tendency to become obsessed with plans and objectives. I had spent a lifetime wasting that energy on my gambling efforts. This would be my first opportunity to "put the enemy to work." My plan was to cold call the entire building. There was a small chance I could find a new client.

My sales manager, a very sweet Irish lady named Mary Deegan, had given me some advice that morning while she walked me over to the corner of 42nd and Lexington Avenue. She said, "Just be yourself, and let the people find the winner inside you". I smiled at her. I said "I feel a bit on edge" She nodded. "That is good, learn to use that energy".

She was like a mother taking her child to school for the first day. She had been the same lady that had interviewed me for the job at Temp Positions, and she had explained to the higher-ups at the company that despite my having absolutely no sales experience, she had a feeling that I would be an outstanding sales representative if I was only given an opportunity. I did not want to let Mary down, and I resolved to do my very best that day.

The Chrysler building has seventy-seven floors and felt like the tallest building in the world. I did not know how to start. So, I decided to start on the top floor of the building and work my way down. My anxiety changed to excitement as the elevator ascended.

When I knocked on my first door, an older white lady opened it. She was maybe in her 50s, and soft-spoken. She said, "Good afternoon. May I help you?"

I replied, "Yes! Good afternoon, I'm Michael Williams with a company called Temp Positions. I was hoping to give you some information about our employment and staffing services. Is there anyone I can speak to just for a few moments?" I spoke so quickly that I am not sure she understood what I had said.

The lady was rather polite. She told me, "I'll take the information, but we are not looking to hire anyone right now. We're a small company with mainly part-time workers."

"That's okay," I said, "I'd like to give you my card and my brochure, and please keep in mind that we don't charge a fee if you're not pleased with the person that you hire."

After she shut the door, I exhaled. I was thinking I could do this. Then I knocked on the next door. This time was an older white man answered the door. "Yes? What is it?"

I became a bit nervous. I began my spiel, "I'm Michael Williams with Temp Positions. My company provides employees and I have information about hiring—"

He cut me off before I finished my sentence. "No, no, I'm too busy now! I'm not hiring. Goodbye!"

Slam! He quickly shut the door.

I froze for a moment, staring at the door. A voice in my head told me, "Snap out of it! Let's get going!" So I moved onto the next door and knocked again. For the rest of the afternoon, door after door, my calls ended with someone slamming the door in my face. Each time I was thinking maybe the next one. I was having some mixed feelings. It was like I was chasing again.

I started to think that I was in the wrong business. These sales calls were more difficult than I had expected. I started to think about the OTB, where picking out a horse was much easier than this. However, I reminded myself that the horses I picked never came in.

It was a waste of time. I now have a real job. I had to confront my emotions and push forward.

It was coming to the end of the afternoon and it was almost time to go back and meet Mary at the Temp Positions office. I had knocked on over a hundred doors that afternoon and I had collected twenty-five business cards, which we call leads. There was always the chance that if I called these cards, I could get a person on the phone and they might want to hire someone. Callbacks were what my job was all about.

I decided to knock on one more door before leaving. It was a travel agency office. Again, an older white lady opened the door and asked if she could help me. Tiredly, I replied, "I'm Michael Williams from Temp Positions. I was hoping to speak to someone about any available jobs."

For a moment she seemed puzzled. She asked me, "Are you looking for a job?"

"No, no," I quickly responded, "I'm offering to connect you with candidates." She hesitated again, and then she said, "We are looking for a part-time file clerk."

My heart began to pound in my chest. It looked like I had just found my first client. I felt adrenaline rush through my body, just like that feeling at the racetrack. But this action was different; it was all about making a sale.

I did my best to remain calm and speak slowly. I told her, "I'd be very happy to provide you with some resumes if you give me your name and phone number. I will call you as I get back to my office."

She gave me her business card and told me she'd share more details about the job description when I called. As I reached up to take the card, my hands were shaking. I thanked her very much for taking the time to speak to me. I promised to call later that afternoon. I smiled at her, and she smiled back at me. I turned and walked back to the elevator, barely containing the pep in my step. I almost wanted to run back to my office.

Back at my office, I immediately went to see Mary so I could tell her about my first day. I found her sitting at her desk reading a newspaper. Mary had her own small office with a nice view of the city, and she always had flowers on her desk. My cubicle was a few feet away from all of the other sales representatives.

Mary smiled at me as I walked in the door. "How was your first day in the field?" she asked me. "I always suggest the Chrysler building as a start for new sales reps. It is a large building so you have lots of offices to check out. You can go back a few more times this week so you can cover the whole building."

I asked permission to sit down, and I took out the stack of business cards. I said, "Actually, I completed the building today, and I have almost twenty-five business cards in my pocket. Also, I think I have my first client. A travel agency needs a part-time file clerk."

Mary looked astonished. She said, "Are you telling me you got a new client on your first day? Did you say you called on one hundred companies this afternoon? That's remarkable! I don't know how you did it, but it sounds like you are going to do very well here."

This was perhaps the first time that Mary had hired someone with an obsessive-compulsive personality. I was not fully aware of what was happening myself. I was learning that when the obsession is productively channeled, it can take a person in an entirely new direction. My affliction was turning into an asset. The rush of adrenaline that I felt as I approached each cold call continued to help me.

For the average salesperson, the feeling is the opposite. Most look forward to making the last call so they can go home. In my case, I always wanted to make one more call before I left for the day, the same way that I had always wanted to make one more bet before I left the casino.

I had always seen myself as a single guy, not the type to settle down. Just like my mother, I did not have much luck with relationships. However, I was beginning to struggle with isolation.

It was strange. I had stopped gambling, and now experienced a different type of loneliness. I decided to get out and meet people, hopefully, a young lady.

First, I dated a young lady from work. Donna was not only beautiful, but she was also funny. We when out to clubs, we both loved music and dancing. I wanted the relationship to grow. Yet, I still struggled with the ability to trust another person. It did not work out too well. After a few months, she stopped calling.

Then, my younger sister Susan invited me to a barbecue at her house, it would be a family reunion. There I met the young lady to whom I would later get married. Sally was also born in the Bronx and was Puerto Rican. She had lived for a few years in one of the group homes for girls in Staten Island, where she met my sister Susan.

Incidentally, that reunion was also the last time that most of the family ever saw Gary. I took a family picture that I often look at today. I call it the reunion that "almost never was," because Gary would be dead three months later.

After that reunion, I decided I wanted to be with Sally. Unfortunately, I had reached the point where trust was a big issue. That is not a good way to start a relationship. Also, it was becoming very difficult for me to ignore the fact that I was not ready to get involved in a relationship or start a family. Yet, I really wanted to believe that I was in love, and I had every hope for a happy life. So I decided I would give it my best shot.

And, for a brief moment, I was actually happy.

Sally and I decided to move in together pretty quickly. We got a place on Daniel Low Terrace in Staten Island. We had only known each other for a few months when she told me that a child was on the way. She was in complete shock and was thinking about getting an abortion. I told her that was insane and that I thought we should get married. So instead of having a depressing conversation about abortion, we walked over to a place on 41st Street and Madison Avenue called "The President" and ordered a bottle of champagne to celebrate. I felt like a big-shot.

Sally already had a little girl named Juleah, and she became my first daughter. Nine months later my daughter Maxine came into the world. I was both excited, and nervous about becoming a father. Because I had grown up without a father, I had no real concept of what "being a father" meant. I looked around and found very few good examples of what a real father looks like. In the beginning, I had no role model. My older brothers would simply impregnate a woman and leave. In my view, that was not an example of fatherhood. That was being what one woman referred to as "a sperm donor." I was determined to never be just a "sperm donor," and I was committed to my family, determined to be a real father for Juleah and Maxine. To me, it was the most important commitment I ever made. I now had a family.

To me, this was heaven. I had a beautiful wife and now two beautiful girls. I had a decent job; however, I needed to earn more money. Still, I felt fortunate. I continue to re-read my books. I tried to follow all the principles of motivation and positive thinking.

Looking back, my marriage was an example of what I would later call "the self-sabotage trap" and "the big shot syndrome." To a certain extent, I set myself up to fail. A good example was how we started. We planned a wedding knowing full well I had no money, and yet had a wedding with one hundred and eighty-five guests. We paid for all the expenses with Visa and MasterCard. How many people do you know who would have a wedding and put the whole thing on plastic? Yet, for one day, I felt like a king. For one night I was "Gatsby". We had the best food, drinks, and I really enjoyed the music. And, the pictures looked great too.

One month after we returned home from our honeymoon, the credit card statements started to arrive. In a way, the marriage was over before the honeymoon, and I'm amazed we lasted two more years. These were all signs of the compulsive gambling mentality, of wanting the good things in life without making the real effort to achieve the goals that are part of the whole.

Yet, I wanted to take care of my family. I was back to working six days a week and I worked like the devil. However, my wife did not see it that way. One day she told me, "You loser! We can't even pay our bills!" She took my two girls and moved away, which broke my heart. I was thinking about taking a chance with gambling again.

At New York Port Authority one afternoon, I heard a song by Lou Rawls, "You Will Never Find Another Love Like Mine," playing in the background. It fit my frame of mind at that time. When the marriage collapsed, I fell into a dark place. I started thinking about Atlantic City again. I remembered the lights and the free drinks at the casino. I could hear that old demon calling me back.

When I got married, my good friend Tony was my best man. Then, we all flew to the Dominican Republic. They had gifted me and my new wife a *villa* for a whole week as a wedding present. The four of us went out on the town.

On the second day of our vacation, we were all driving back to the house from a city called Bonao. It had been a really beautiful day. Tony looked over at Raquel and said, "Hey sweetheart, let's go get married."

I looked at Tony, and said, "Are you serious? You're gonna get married wearing swimming trunks?"

Tony just smiled and looked at me with his cigar in his mouth, doing an impression of Carmine Galante. He said, "Why not? We've been talking about it for years, and this is a great place to get married." Then he asked, "Mike, will you be my best man?" I could not help but laugh. We stopped at a courthouse, and I watched Tony and Racquel get married. They paid fifteen pesos for the marriage license.

That was almost thirty years ago, and Tony and Racquel are still married today. Sure, they've had their share of challenges but are still together, and only spent fifteen pesos. So, I paid for a wedding that I could not afford, I charged the wedding on at least ten different credit cards, and two years later my wife had walked out.

You do not have to be a genius to know that charging your wedding on your credit cards is possibly the dumbest way to start a marriage. The signs of self-sabotage could not have been more obvious. However, I found it easier to live in denial, which can be just as powerful as addiction. I knew that I had work to do. I had to face the man in the mirror.

KEEP THE FAITH

By 1990, the world was changing, and so was New York City. I read in a newspaper that Nelson Mandela had walked out of a jail after 27 years. In New York City, we elected a man named David Dinkins as mayor. The first time a black man was ever elected Mayor of New York City. Mayor Dinkins had a strong impact on my perception of being a black man. Yet, I read about another mayor, Marion Barry. He was arrested smoking crack in a hotel in Washington, DC. A reminder of the power of addiction. One night, I watched Mike Tyson get knocked out by a guy named Buster Douglas, and I read about a fire in a social club called "Happy Land" That fire killed 87 people.

I had my own problems. My marriage had failed. For some reason, I wanted to take a trip to Atlantic City. That was the place to go to get rid of the pain. Yet, I knew deep in my heart I did not want to go back to gambling, and I was sure nothing good could come of it. But, that old demon was in my ear again. He was calling me.

So, I instead reached out to my friend Bernie P. from my recovery group, and I read my books again. I had become a follower of motivational teachings. I gave copies of these books to other people as gifts. I learned that recovery was a gift, however, the only way to keep it was to give it away. So, I handed out books by Napoleon Hill to the young men at the group homes. I bought into everything that I read in these books.

I also found my higher power on the road to recovery. I began attending the weekend retreat at St. Ignatius in Long Island, and Mount Manresa in Staten Island. I met a lot of good men at those retreats, but more importantly, I developed a relationship with God. I look for people everywhere, and always love to talk about the power of God Almighty. These days, I sometimes talk with my neighbor, Glenn, who always provided some valuable insights about the spiritual journey we find ourselves on.

So, I did not run to Atlantic City. I did go to the movies. My favorite movies that year were "Goodfellas", "Pretty Woman" and "Ghost". I watched "King of New York" quite a few times. It was a difficult time, and yet I was determined to stay on track. It was time to "act as if".

I finally began to believe the story my mother told me about the three angels praying over me as a baby. They poured water all over my little body and prayed for me. Did they bless me?

I believed that was why I survived that night at the TipTop Lounge, and the other nights when I could have lost my life. So, I would continue to attend retreats for the next three decades, and I would learn to believe that I was protected from above. I also learn something important about seeking opportunities.

In one of his books, Napoleon Hill talks about something called "the sly disguise of opportunity." Hill believed that opportunity can come at the lowest point of one's life. That is why a person must remain alert: so they can seize the opportunity. In the depths of my despair about my failed marriage, I was about to experience this concept of "the sly disguise of opportunity"

For example, two months after my wife took my two kids and left, I got a phone call from my good friend Phil Baumgarten, another guy from my support group. We also played basketball together. Phil was my accountant, a CPA, and a lawyer, a real down-to-earth guy who happened to be Jewish. Phil wanted to grab lunch the next day, so we met for pizza and soft drinks. He was the first to believe in me.

I told him about Sally leaving with my kids, and how I was a little bit down. I also told him about what was happening at work. The temp agency where I was working had promoted me to the sales manager position. Now, I was opening new accounts all over the place. However, the company did not have any real structure, so I was not only the sales manager but also the office manager, the accounts manager, the collection department, and I did my own recruiting. All while I was generating millions of dollars a year for the company!

Phil thought about this for a moment and asked me, "Wouldn't it make more sense for you to be the owner?" I started to laugh because I didn't think Phil understood the employment business. It takes real capital and resources to operate an agency. The agency required that first, you pay the workers and then collect the fees. So I told Phil it was a nice thought but it would take a lot of money. I knew that Phil did not have a lot of money, and of course, I was completely broke.

However, I was mistaken in my assumption. Indeed, Phil did not have any money. But, he was an accountant and did people's taxes, so he knew which of his clients had money.

Phil said, "Don't laugh, Mike. I know a group of guys who could become our investment team and provide you the resources you need to start your own company." I became quiet.

As a sales manager working for the agency, I was earning only 5% of sales. Phil explained that the investment group would likely want 10% of the gross sales, which would leave me with 90%.

I was in shock. Phil had the math cold. He understood and was serious, he was the first to believe that I could do great things. I looked at Phil and said, "Let's do it."

Even more amazing, I would be able to start a new company, with a full list of clients, and employees. Everyone could follow me out the door. While working for the staffing agency, I did not have a contract to provide me with any security. This made it easier for the company to terminate me. However, it also allowed me to recruit their clients because, without a contract, I had never signed what is known as a nondisclosure agreement (NDA) or a non-compete (NC). That meant that when I walked out the door, I could carry all of my clients and employees with me. Which is what I did.

Two weeks later Phil called me and said that the investment team had agreed to provide financing for the new company. We named ourselves United Personnel Agency, Inc. Phil told me to meet him at Chase Bank that Tuesday morning. On March 26, 1991, I walked into Chase Bank to sign the articles of incorporation, and I signed my name to the bank accounts. At that moment I became Michael Williams, President of United Personnel Agency, Inc. Soon, I was providing staffing services to Merrill Lynch, Bank of New York, and several large employee unions in New York City. It was also the anniversary of the day my mom died.

I later met an individual named Bill Reel who was a writer for New York Newsday. He also knew me from the support group. He felt my story was important and he wrote five articles for the paper about this homeless man who became the owner of an employment agency.

Bill and I developed a great friendship. We enjoyed talking about recovery, and I told him stories about my journey. I shared with him the books that had influenced my life. We also talked about United Personnel Agency, and I told Bill how my agency was growing.

One year, I generated over $2 million in sales. In 1994, I mailed out three hundred and twenty-eight W-2 forms to my employees. I hadn't even known that I had employed so many individuals! My agency was now generating real profits, and I was feeling like I was on top of the world.

Oddly, once I became CEO of my own staffing agency, my ex-wife wanted to reunite. However, I knew that trust was still a big issue with me. I did not want someone to be with me just for the good times; I needed someone to be with me when I was catching hell, too. If I ever married again, I wanted to believe that I'd found the kind of person who would be with me for better or worse, during good times and bad, and in sickness and in health. I never did find that person, and so I never remarried. However, once I was pretty close.

I took my responsibilities as a father very seriously. I felt very fortunate to have been given joint custody and I did not miss any visits with my kids, even when I was sick. I rationalized that if I was still married, I would see my kids even if I had a cold. So I never called Sally to say, "I can't pick up the kids today for this weekend." To me, that was just an excuse, the easy way out.

This was also a very important time of learning for me. People like Ron, Mickey, Dave S., Jeff G., Irwin S., and Bill R. taught me real-life lessons. These lessons had more meaning for me now than ever before. I also had my books, which was a wealth of knowledge. I read Robert Ringer's book *Looking Out for Number One.* For the first time in my life, I experienced a sense of empowerment. One day I was sleeping in the streets, living as a scavenger, and the next I was a successful business owner. I was hopeful and encouraged that I would achieve the goals written on my one-year, five-year, and ten-year plans.

I was full of exhilaration and anticipation. I also had a great deal of fear because deep inside me there was still a compulsive gambler. I still didn't know enough about self-sabotage and self-doubt, but I knew my tendency for self-destruction.

What would happen over the next few months and years would teach me a great deal more. But, for the first time in a long time, I had something to hold onto the promise of a better tomorrow. For the first time in my life, I knew what I was living for.

My mother Ruth Hearns Williams, age 17, arrived from Birmingham

A Mother's Love, Photo taken by me, on her last birthday (Age40) died three months later

My 6th grade graduation picture, Michael (Age 12) four months after the death of my mother Ruth.

It was a 50 year search for this Photo; My father John Henry Jarvis, Jr.

My second year at the Richmond Hill Group Home for Boys, I was selected for CYO St. Theresa's team (Age 14) One of the starting five – SG. None of the other boys made the team. Our house parents that year were Mr. and Mrs. James Harris (we called him Mr. Hook) here with one of the home boys, Carlos Torres.

My Father John Henry Jarvis, Jr. and his family (my aunt, Irene, Etta, my Dad John, my grandmother Ella, aunt Charlotte, uncles William, and James)

Thanks to DNA technology and Maxine, I not only learned about my real father John Jarvis, I learned about his family too, including my great grandmother, Jennie Cailey, a white lady, born on Isle of Man, in the UK, who married a former slave, Edward Jarvis. They had a son, my grandfather. John Jarvis, Sr

Mary A. James - my other mother.

From Gambler (1982- the Tiptop Lounge) to Sales Rep-Executive (1985- Tempositions, Inc.) here with Mary Diehgan looking on.

Me (Father, and Businessman) and my Girls, Maxine & Juleah.

On the campaign with my daughter Maxine.

My Maxine, The delegate from New York

Maxine working with Hillary 2016 for President of the United States

Hanging with The Hall of Fame Legend Bernard King.

At MSG with Knick's Legend John Starks and Dr. Dick Barnett.

Joined with Dick Barnett, to support Senator Bill Bradley in his bid for President of the United States, also met filmmaker, Spike Lee.

The First WBA Basketball camp at John Jay College, me with Dick Barnett

The WBA Grand Reception on opening night with the NBA Legends (Cal Ramsey, Dick Barnett, Luther Rackley, Dean Meminger, Earl Monroe).

The WBA Basketball Camps at John Jay College guided by my mentor Dick Barnett.

A friend and colleague Dean "the Dream" Meminger- Running the first WBA Camp.

The WBA Basketball Teams, with help from the NY Liberty's Kim Hampton.

At the WBA Reception with Phil Baumgarten (My good friend, CPA and first to believe in the dream).

With one and only Mr. Cool -Walt Clyde Frazier @ the Wine and Dine.

My Friend and Mentor; The Legend- Earl "The Pearl" Monroe.

The Family Reunion with our Aunt Grace (my mom's older sister).

The last family reunion with my brother Gary (Dangerous) Williams (white hat) Juan, Frank, Nat, Gary, Susan, Ruth, Michael, Christine, & Barbara (we lost Barbara to cancer a few years later).

Me and Baby Brother," - Gregory Williams – Once lost, now found.

Birthday for Barbara, with my brothers, including Frank (on the end, in checker shirt) he died a few years later, age 37.

The First Born; My brother Harold Lewis, (gave me my first lesson in self-confidence) Unfortunately, he died at age 26.

My brother Richard (Alcatraz) Williams at Attica State Prison, selected for the men's basketball team, He should have been at Rucker's that summer. He served a life sentence.

My brother Gary (Dangerous) Williams, who met my mentor Ron (The Jeweler) Davis. Gary died three months later age 32.

Prodigal Son, My brother Richard (now, Abdul Ali) returns home after 25 year term in prison and meets my grandson Jayden, who shows him how to use a laptop.

My Birthday Party, with friends John Starks, Jeannie, Jason, and Walt III.

Ready for the virtual graduation ceremony, and thinking " you come a long way baby".

PART TWO

CHAPTER 4

"I have a dream that one day I will live in a nation where I will not be judged by the color of my life, but by the content of my character"

Dr. Martin Luther King, Jr

KEY TO THE FIVE C'S

It was 1991, and my world was changing, and for the better. I was operating my own company, United Personnel Agency, Inc. At times I had hundreds of people on my payroll. I was controlling millions of dollars every year. But I struggled to adjust to my new way of life. I felt like I was walking on thin ice, and I seemed to always live on the edge. It was like I was not comfortable with success.

Yet, I was given a serious warning from someone in my recovery group. He said, "It will not matter how much money you make, or what new job you find. Your only chance for a better life depends on you making character changes". I was told that if I did not change my character, I was doomed. In some ways, I still had the character of the gambler, despite the changes in my life. Accepting change in my life was my biggest challenge.

I read a story about a serial killer, this time, a woman. Her name was Aileen Wuornos. I watched the start of the Gulf War on television. For the first time, the stock market hit 3,000. Later that year, Mike Tyson was arrested for rape. Yes, the world was in motion, and the power of addiction was as clear as ever. I still had some of my own demons to face.

First, I struggled with the reality of how to operate my own company. I still felt like I was unworthy of a better life. I call it the "*Twelve Years a Slave*" syndrome. What does that mean? For all of my working life, I always had a boss. From my first day, when my mother took me by the hand to the pharmacist on the corner of 145th and Willis Avenue, I had always worked for somebody, and it had always been a white man.

I was always looking up to hear, what should I do now? Now, I woke up in the morning and went to work, I walked into my office and had nobody to report to. I felt like something was missing. Now, for the first time in my life, I did not have a master. I could not get it in my head that I was truly my own boss. *I own the company*. I needed to repeat it to myself.

To add to that, some of my old demons returned to visit me. Now, I had millions of dollars at my fingertips. Many days I struggled with the urge to gamble. I dreamed about finally taking my first trip to Las Vegas. I could write a check from my payroll account and get on the flight with tens of thousand dollars in my pocket. It was the ultimate fantasy, and it was difficult to suppress my desire. It was also crazy.

It didn't make sense, it was insane, and yet I had to fight it.

During my first few weeks of running United Personnel Agency, I called Phil every few hours and before I made any important decisions. He finally got fed up. He said, "Dammit, Mike, you need to stop calling me! This is *your* company. *You* are the owner. I'm just your accountant. Let me do my work and leave me the hell alone." Click! He hung up on me.

I stood astonished for a moment. Then I realized he was right. I was playing out the old mythology, "Twelve years a slave". I was struggling with the fact that I did not have a white man telling me what to do. That was the last time anyone hung up the phone on me regarding a decision that I needed to make. Now, I became a compulsive decision-maker.

I took charge of my life after that moment, and I was finally able to break the cycle of "the slave-master mentality." I had to make myself understand that I was the boss now. I was the captain of my ship, and I was a master of my soul. However, it also became a time for me to double down on my support groups, and on the people that I looked to for leadership. Fortunately, I had met a few individuals who each provided leadership, and one man, in particular, became a mentor.

That individual was Dr. Dick Barnett. Some people know of him, and some do not. For me, he was a legend. Dick Barnett had a long, fifteen-plus-year career as a star on the basketball court. His college career as a star player for Tennessee State made him a legend before he was even drafted into the NBA. They were an all-black team that went on to win three consecutive championships and was eventually inducted into the Naismith Basketball Hall of Fame in Springfield.

Barnett was the team leader who was there for the induction ceremony. He was also one of the most integral parts of the New York Knick's 1970 world championship team, and perhaps the most overlooked player of the starting five. He won a second championship with the Knicks in 1973.

By the time I met Dick Barnett, he was retired from basketball and was involved with his nonprofit organization. He also mentioned to me briefly during our first meeting that he was considering pursuing a Ph.D. I was fascinated that a retired basketball player would return to school.

I remembered Dick Barnett quite well from when I was a young boy growing up in South Jamaica, Queens. He was the oldest of the New York Knicks and a legend in my neighborhood. I remember how everybody cheered for him when he came off the bench. Naturally, the following day, I would try to imitate his famous "Fall Back Baby" jump-shot in the playgrounds. Amazingly, I did not end up in the hospital. Most guys who tried either ended up hurting their backs or their pride.

One day back in 1988, I was passing by the Pan Am building on 42nd Street and Park Avenue, and I noticed a familiar face hiding behind a New York Times. Immediately, I recognized my old basketball hero, Dick Barnett! I approached him to exchange business cards. I had no idea if I would ever talk with him again, but I knew I would certainly give him a call. There followed a real lesson about persistence and trusting your instincts. At first, Barnett was extremely difficult to reach. I felt like I was trying to contact a ghost. I left countless messages for him on his answering service, and after a while, I gave up hope of ever getting a return call.

By early 1991, we connected. One afternoon my phone rang, and it was Dick Barnett. He wanted to know how I was doing in business. He wanted to talk about the economy and the job market. I was just happy to be talking to him a second time. I wanted to talk about my years growing up and how I would try to copy his jump shot.

We arranged to meet at a café next door to the YMCA on 47th Street. The YMCA restaurant had a cafeteria-style design. The tables were small, almost cubicle-like. There was also a counter where you could sit and eat, or just have coffee. I arrived early and took a table at the end of the restaurant because there was more room to move the chairs away from the table. To my surprise, only a few minutes later the legend himself walked in the door. We ordered lunch and started talking.

At first, we talked mainly about business, the first of many such discussions. However, as the conversation progressed, Barnett began to reminisce about his early years as a youth. I learned from him that his early years were very difficult. Growing up in Gary, Indiana, his family was very poor and at times there was not enough food to eat.

His prospects for the future were not very bright either, and he talked about his concern that he would end up in the coal mines. He realized early on that he had some skills with a basketball, and he knew that was his ticket out of the world of poverty. As a kid, he practiced shooting a ping-pong ball into a tin cup. He was a loner who embraced isolation. In some ways, I felt like I was in the company of another gambler. As a gambler, you learn to accept isolation.

Then we started talking about his work. Barnett operated a nonprofit organization called Athletic Role Models, Inc. (ARM), and most of the programs targeted young, black men who were at risk. At the time, I was twenty-nine years old and had a background that fit quite well with these young men.

Barnett learned that I had experienced real challenges and that I had made a turnaround. He knew that I was now a business owner. So, we made a great connection. Barnett soon began to invite me to be a guest speaker at his programs. At first, it was difficult for me to speak before a group. However, over time, I improved. Soon, I was involved in most of Barnett's programs and motivational workshops.

One important lesson I learned from Barnett was about developing confidence. I observed how he approached a group during a workshop or motivational session. His commanding presence seemed to hypnotize the group.

Barnett also taught me about dedication. For Barnett, that started at the very beginning when he was a young basketball player in high school. No one spent more time on the court working to perfect their game. The dedication was something that he carried over and applied to other endeavors.

Most importantly, Dick Barnett taught me about the Five C's, which are five key principles he taught to the young men involved in his programs at his nonprofit organization. I could see that I had to incorporate those principles into my plans to make more progress in my life and be a leader in my own world. Five C's are: *Conceive. Courage. Commitment. Consistency. Control.* These key lessons would follow me for a lifetime.

First, Dr. Barnett taught that it is important to be able to **conceive.** All too often he found that young men did not have a vision for the future.

At first, I didn't understand the importance of having the ability to conceive. Then I remembered Napoleon Hill's statement that "Whatever the mind of man can conceive and believe, it can achieve." I connected that mantra to the importance of having a vision. I realized that I was doing things I could have only dreamed of years prior because I had had a vision, and had used the principles of motivation to pursue that vision. It had been important for me to visualize myself taking on challenges and handling my responsibility.

Next, Dr. Barnett explained the importance of having the **courage** to follow that vision. So often a person can create a vision but not have the courage to pursue it. For me, it was the start of my own company United Personnel Agency. I had to make the jump. I had to have faith.

Then, courage must be combined with **commitment**. It is not enough to be brave for a day. The effort must be sustained. The first year was very difficult, and I almost gave up on the new company. So, I had to learn about commitment. I had to invest my soul in the journey.

Achieving a dream also requires **consistency.** A person might commit themselves to their goals but then stop and start along the way. I had to develop a system. I needed some order in my life. I had to learn to do the right thing and follow up at the right time.

Finally, Dr. Barnett taught his students that they must demonstrate **control.** Dr. Barnett made this point much more strongly than all the others. So many people go the distance to achieve their goals only to lose control at the end—like my idea of taking a trip to Las Vegas, after finally building a successful company. That would have been a disaster. Yet, I had found success to be a double-edged sword. On the one hand, so many people start a new business and fail. On the other hand are people like me, who came from the gutter and who rarely enjoyed any type of life beyond subsistence. So, blessed with success for the first time, it's easy to give in to that temptation.

Like so many who had never tasted success before, these principles were challenging for me. I had reached the point where I could live out my dreams, and consistency and control did not fit. This is not a rare phenomenon. Many people who achieved success in the public eye have struggled with control—Mike Tyson, Evander Holyfield, and Allen Iverson. Many people are not aware that people like MC Hammer, Toni Braxton, Burt Reynolds, Michael Jackson, Donald Trump, and 50 Cent all went bankrupt. This phenomenon of losing control can result in some very hard lessons. So, I needed to understand that control was the key to everything.

I knew that for me to achieve my goals, I had to embrace the principles of the Five C's. During my first year as CEO and President of United Personnel Agency, I also struggled to keep my ego in check, a struggle I often took for granted. I had to recognize my persistent need to win over and be accepted by other people.

In the case of United Personnel Agency, not only was I growing the company too fast, but I also had problems managing resources. I was the sole owner and operator of the entire company.

To add to some of the challenges, my daughter Maxine told me that she wanted to move to New York, and live with me. I agreed, and after a few difficult conversations with my ex-wife, we made the move. Now, I am a full-time Dad. I have my own company, and my little girl lives with me. I paid off my investors and now owned the company 100%. So, I was also the only decision-maker. Keeping my ego in check was a balancing act.

As my company became bigger and more successful, and as I began handling millions of dollars, I found myself putting on parties and affairs for friends, colleagues, and family members. These were a mix of business and celebration—the lines were a little bit hazy. I was having difficulty accepting my success in life. I was not consistent, because at times I changed my plans on a whim.

I was not in control, because I still needed to win friends and influence people. I still had my struggles with my ego and what I call "the big shot syndrome". Once again, like the old gambler I was, I wanted to live in my dream world. Somehow, I was finally in a relationship with a nice lady. May was from Africa. A place called Senegal. For the first time, I really felt good in a relationship. Yet, I was restless. I was still unsure of myself. We broke up a year later.

My memories of 2001, focused on the events of September 11, I had scheduled a business meeting that morning next door to One World Trade Center. My client called me at 8.55 AM. She told me that we need to cancel our appointment. I could not imagine what she was seeing from her office window. Sadly, I found myself thinking about running to Atlantic City. Instead, I made arrangements to help some of my employees.

By 2002, I convinced myself that business was great. So, I bought myself a brand-new Mercedes-Benz, even though I'm a terrible driver. I bought the car because I was a single man and a divorced father who was trying to meet women. One of the most annoying questions that women would ask me was, "What type of car do you drive?" At first, I would answer, "I live in Manhattan so I don't need a car." Not exactly an answer that impresses a lady.

So I bought myself the Benz. The car was very expensive and I did not drive it much at all. I did sometimes pick up my daughter Maxine from school after her basketball games. She told me that I was such a terrible, slow driver, she'd prefer to take the train instead.

However, the Mercedes-Benz was still beautiful to look at, and so I drove it to the car wash two blocks from my house once a week. I didn't understand a lot about cars. One day I got a flat tire and drove the car back to the dealership. They fixed the tire and charged me $350.00. Remember, this was in 2002. There was a repair shop five blocks from my house that fixed flat tires for $15.

Another time, the car completely shut down on the highway. In a rage, I called the car dealership again, screaming that my brand-new car had just broken down. They sent a pickup truck to bring me back to the dealership. There, the mechanic examined the car carefully. Finally, he found the problem.

"You're out of gas."

"Oh, okay," I said, "I just need to go to the gas station and get gas?"

The mechanic promised that if I put some gas in the car, it would run perfectly.

"Oh," I replied, looking at the wall, "I guess that makes sense."

This is funny in retrospect, but at the time it was pathetic. Clearly, I had to learn some basic things.

I also took extravagant trips every year. Each time, I treated a group of twelve to fourteen people to a vacation that involved the purchase of their airline tickets and their tickets for a cruise. As you can imagine, these were very expensive vacations. One could argue that I should have taken a minute to remember where I was in 1982: "*homeless*". Yet, I acted like it was no big deal. It was all about boosting my ego now.

I loved the idea of taking my two daughters on a cruise. So, we planned a few trips. I also invited my sister Susan and my niece Tamara, and my brother Juan and my nephew, Harold. Then I invited a good friend, Fred, who I had known since the seventh grade. Fred was not only a great friend for many years but was also the manager at the law firm Latham & Watkins. One of his responsibilities was to hire people for temporary jobs.

When I first told Fred that I was starting my own company, he was even more excited than I was. He directed all his job openings to United Personnel Agency and became one of my first and most important clients. He was a truly great friend, and we still enjoy the occasional reunion to have a drink and talk about old times.

These vacations were great, and I even had the pleasure of meeting Meli'sa a well-known singer. The people loved her music, and some great relationships emerged. It was great to walk into the lounge with Meli'sa, and hear the DL playing "Fool's Paradise" She even introduced my daughter Maxine to a young man, whom she later married. I met many people on these vacations, and so I justified the trip as opportunities for networking and developing relationships.

However, I was out of touch with reality. My company was experiencing some real management challenges back in New York, and yet, I was enjoying champagne on a cruise with my family and friends. This was an example of self-sabotage.

So, understanding the five C's was also an educational process, though it didn't come with a diploma or graduation date. I must admit that when I look back on those years, I see where I should have done some things differently.

I'll also note that I don't regret everything that happened on those expensive vacations because it was on one of those vacations that my daughter Maxine, who was thirteen at the time, met a young boy her age and they exchanged phone numbers. The young boy lived in Bermuda, but they stayed in touch, writing each other letters and talking on the phone. FaceTime did not exist then. They met only once or twice that entire time. Yet, five years later, they got married. It was a classic love story. Now they have two children. My granddaughter Arianna reminds me of my daughter and has given me much love and sunlight in my life. A few years later, my grandson Jayden was born.

My daughter thinks that we look alike, me and my grandson. I can only tell you that he is the absolute joy of my life. When he puts his arms around my neck and says, "Grandpa, I love you," I know that the love is real. It is not like my phony days when I was a gambler trying to buy friends and win the love of strangers.

Similarly, when I visit my daughter Juleah and get to see my granddaughter Tatyanna and my grandson Dayden, I know it's real, not the phony nonsense that I remember from my years talking to drunks in a bar. Drunks always love each other at 3 am.

Oddly enough, I recognize that the "I love you" is what I was chasing the whole time I was a sick, compulsive gambler. So, I cannot regret too much those expensive vacations, even though I spent more money than I should.

However, I knew that my recovery was on the line. I am still a compulsive gambler at heart. My only chance at a better way of life is by making real changes- character changes. It is a difficult process and a life-long pursuit. I needed to take real steps towards making character changes within myself.

Otherwise, no amount of money could save me from me. I would soon meet some of the people who would help me to find the right path.

I met a woman. Elizabeth. To me, this was the real deal. I fell head over heels. Now, remember that I had waited seven years after the end of my first marriage before even considering another relationship, but now I decided it was time to get remarried.

I was still feeling pretty pessimistic after my first marriage. I had to come to terms with the fact that I would likely never really trust anyone in that way ever again. However, some people believe that time can heal all wounds. I wanted to believe that as well. So when I met Elizabeth, I tried to believe that I had changed. I now had the opportunity to start a new chapter in my life. I wanted to believe in happiness. I wanted to believe that I had met the woman of my dreams. Yet, trust is a big deal, and I had problems with trust even before I met my first wife.

Elizabeth was everything I ever wanted in a woman. She was a beautiful lady with the face of a movie star. She reminded me of Josephine Baker, the famous singer of the 1930s. Her smile and laugh were infectious. Elizabeth also loved to dance, she loved dancing in the living room nude for me. I felt like I was back at the strip club. We met at a place on 51th Street, and Third Ave in Manhattan. It was the "Friday Happy Hour" at Le Magenet. We hit it off right away. The next weekend, she stayed at my place on Roosevelt Island.

At the time I was working seven days a week and I had a sense that I was entitled to enjoy my life. So we decided to do some traveling. Elizabeth and I traveled to different places together, including a trip to Paris. We went to parties and we vacationed with friends: My good friends Al and Jackie would join us for a quick trip to Springfield, Massachusetts to our summer house. We would vacation in Jamaica, or Puerto Rico.

For Elizabeth's birthday, I rented out a catering hall and tried to capture the feeling of my favorite movie, *Casablanca*. I wore my white tuxedo and held my cigarette like Humphrey Bogart. Well, let's say Bogart with a really great tan.

We were doing it all, and once again I felt like I was living my dream—this time, without gambling! I felt like I had earned my rewards, and so imagined that I wasn't falling into any of my old traps. However, even this was all just a page out "the big shot syndrome" playbook.

The fact was that once again I was trying to project an image to a woman. Once again it was the type of relationship that was not sustainable. Once again, my financial situation was not nearly as strong as I made it out to be. I was starting to drink more, and Liz was starting to drink *much* more. Her drinking reached the point of being a problem for me. It was not unusual for me to be home alone all weekend and not get a phone call from her until a few days later.

When Liz did finally call, she would say she was having doubts about the relationship. She would tell me she was doing some soul-searching. Unfortunately, she was talking to a man who had a problem trusting others. I started thinking that she had done more than just soul-searching that weekend. Finally, I realized that I could not marry this woman. We broke off our engagement and she moved into her own apartment in New Jersey. For a brief moment, we thought we might continue seeing each other.

However, we soon realized that was ridiculous. We were engaged to be married in a few months, and yet we were moving into separate apartments. We finally decided to end the relationship. That was the last time I was ever close to any chance at marriage. I do think of Liz from time to time. I never saw or heard from her again after she moved out. I was deeply disappointed, but not thinking about going back to gambling.

I decided to double down with my recovery groups. I was proud of myself for what I had accomplished. So, I did not ever return to gambling, no more casinos or racetracks. I had not made a single bet. However, I needed to do more. It seemed that despite the hard lessons, I had done the right thing regarding my recovery. I had not let the big shot syndrome completely take me down.

I always remind myself of those years as a homeless man sleeping on the streets. It is always best to not forget the journey. To remember the past. I decided to go back to basics and do the things that had allowed me to make progress in the very beginning. I decided to attend more meetings each week and make at least two or three phone calls to other group members every week. It was also time to get back to the weekend recovery retreats. Recovery is a life-long work in progress.

LESSONS OF LEGENDS

I have always been a huge basketball fan. As a kid, my life was changed by a chance meeting with legendary New York Knick's star Cazzie Russell. It was a lesson that I remember to this very day.

I will always remember that meeting. It happened the summer I turned fourteen years old, at a gym in Queens called the Lost Battalion Hall. One afternoon, I found Cazzie there shooting hoops by himself. Cazzie Russell, NBA world champion. A real legend. During his career at Michigan State University, he was considered the best basketball player in the United States. Some remember the classic matchup between Russell and Bill Bradley, who later served as a United States Senator and ran as a candidate for President of the United States.

I just found my way into the gym. However, the place was closed. A door was left open by mistake. I could hear a ball bouncing. I walked in. To my surprise, Cazzie actually took the time to talk to me then. Looking back, I could see that he was trying to make me think about my future. He understood that as a teenage black boy, I would soon make some of the most important decisions of my life. However, Cazzie was clever enough to know that I just wanted to talk about basketball. He used that opportunity of playing ball to teach me some life lessons. Surprisingly, everything he taught me that day, I continued to use for the rest of my life.

First, he taught me how to shoot a basketball. Then he showed me how to shoot from the foul line. That lesson may have helped me make the team at St. Theresa's. Then, Cazzie began talking about life in general and the importance of making decisions. He talked quite a bit about the mistakes young people make. He took time to talk to me about the people we select to be a part of our lives. He warned me to choose my friends carefully. It was a lesson that remains with me to this day.

I decided to share those experiences with homeless men in New York City. We were meeting in the men's shelter auditorium, so I walked down to the bottom floor. There must've been at least three hundred and fifty men waiting in the meeting area. There was hardly any air conditioning on the warm spring evening. The space felt very tight! I was introduced by Dick Barnett. Once I began to speak, however, I felt each man hanging on my words.

I think I got their attention when I began to share my experience of sleeping in the subway night after night.

I talked about my nights sleeping in abandoned buildings, and of course my trips to the racetrack to try to get on top again. These men understood my struggle. I made it clear in no uncertain terms that I had never found a quick and easy way which succeed, and I told them that I had actually been robbing myself of my future. I stressed the importance of finally coming to terms with reality. I talked about the five C's- I talked about the importance of making character changes in life.

Then, when I stepped off the stage, Dick Barnett took the microphone and began speaking.

He described his desire to better his situation in life because his options in Gary, Indiana had been limited. Barnett explained to these men what it took for him to make it into college basketball, and then to prepare for the transition from college to the pros. He also talked about how many men had missed their opportunity because of drugs, alcohol, and gambling.

It was clear that our stories made an impression on the audience. Some of the men changed the direction of their lives that same day. A few of the men wanted to talk with me about how to prepare themselves to get back into the job market. However, I do think that some just gave us lip service and then returned to their old ways of living.

Before Barnett wrapped the meeting up, he added one more thing. He shared a poem that he had written in 1996, titled **"WHAT NOW MY BROTHER."**

What now, my brother?
After the cheering has ended and the applause and accolades begin descending,
What now, my brother?
When the media and the fans turned to others for their dose of the entertainment pill,
When no one notices you and life begins to turn real,
What now, my brother, what happened to the hang-er on?
Did they leave you for another,
Or did they diss you in scorn?

What now, my brother, now that you've left you all along at a time
To repent and reflect and realize that you are finally on your own.

What happened to the cheers and seats packed pack through the years,
People calling your name as you ride the whirlwind of intoxicating drama and fame?
The waiting time has run its course,
The airports are empty and only the ghosts rejoice
As a shadow of the fleeing fame disappears
And the cold reality of the real world finally awakes and sears
The brother who believes the high-octane ride would never end.
As wilting shock of reality will regrettably begin,
Bringing loneliness, tears and gathering jeers
Of the peanut gallery and the loss of super salaries,
What now, my brother?

The investment cupboard is bare.
Did the agents and caretakers take care of themselves?
Did they leave a future that is secure,
Or will you walk along hounded by the wolves?
What now, my brother, as the world closes in on you?
Will they remember you as hero, or will they smile as you stew
In your own disregard for a future that look bright and far
And would never reach the end,
Avoiding frightening thoughts of forced retirement just around the bend.
What now, my brother? Can you adjust to the stillness?
Will dim light bring fulfillment?
Can it meet your emotion and psychological needs,
Or will the stillness sow the frightening seeds
Of self-pity and regret
Clinging in the stillness from not knowing what is coming next?

Have you finished your education? Can you face the aggravation?
Have you developed headaches as you approach the final take?
What, now my brother, now that that it's over?
It was a good long ride,
Cushioned by the exceptional life, intangible achievements and egotistical pride.
What now, my brother, as the curtains come down?
As the television camera utters not a sound?
What now, my brother?
As the pat on the backs no longer exist,
And you walk into another life and bravely insist

That I can adjust, I can do it all by myself,
But the emotional and psychological demands instant and immediate help.
What now, my brother?

As Barnett finished, the room was completely silent. The men seemed hypnotized. They may have been thinking, just as I was, *If someone who was once a basketball player developed such diverse skills, then returned to school, found a new purpose, including becoming a poet, maybe, I can too.*

I continued to watch Barnett as he pushed the envelope. He wanted to make people think about what was possible. So, that same year, 2004, I collaborated with Dr. Barnett to develop the Worldwide Basketball Association. The WBA was a network of former professional basketball players and institutions that provided basketball programs for adults and summer camps for children. For example, during our first year, we worked with John Jay College of Criminal Justice to start a summer camp for youth. Before long, we were working with many other private corporations and community groups. The WBA was really a motivational program. It was about more than basketball. It was really about preparing young people for life in the real world. Our programs were focused on awareness, and avoiding the traps in life.

Many of the student participants in the camps came from very poor families. These young men reported to the camp for the first day, but their parents did not have the money to pay. I could not turn the kids away. So, we allowed a group of fifty kids to attend the summer camp without payment.

These kids had the opportunity to meet NBA legends like Dick Barnett, Earl Monroe, and Dean "The Dream" Meminger. Through Dr. Barnett, I met other members of the 1973 New York Knicks World Championship team. I thereby gained access to a whole network of people, basketball legends, who were connected to that team.

To my surprise, most were really down to earth. Despite the fame and recognition that these guys had experienced, deep down inside they were just like the average person on the street. They had the same concerns, health problems, financial problems, and fears.

In 2004, I talked with Walt "Clyde" Frazier just before the New York Knicks/Boston Celtics game at Madison Square Garden. Even though he was scheduled to begin broadcasting the game in a few minutes, he politely engaged me.

I told him that I once saw him driving his Rolls-Royce out of a parking lot on 57th Street and Second Avenue as I was leaving class at the High School of Art and Design. He was such a hero of mine that I made a drawing of him wearing his number 10 jersey. Clyde took the time to talk to me for a few minutes and then signed my drawing.

Some thirty-five years later, through Barnett's network, I could talk to Clyde Frazier like we were old friends. I wanted him to know that I had always been impressed by his professionalism and dignity. It was no mystery to me why everyone called him "Mr. Cool". From my first meetings with Clyde, I learned so much about the importance of appearance and first impressions. I later became friendly with his son Walt III, and I saw a lot of what I admired in the father in his son.

I also had many conversations with the legend Cal Ramsey, who, after a very brief time with the New York Knicks as a basketball player, enjoyed a long career as a commentator and analyst. Cal was someone I could talk to and get advice from. He was the kind of person that would take the time to help you. If I was hosting an event for my nonprofit or searching for candidates for employment, Cal was my go-to guy. I also found him to be a great help in getting tickets to Knicks games.

Dean "The Dream" Meminger was a good friend. He joined me, along with Dick Barnett to run our summer basketball camp for the first year of the Worldwide Basketball Association. It was one of the best summer camps ever conducted by the league. I was shocked when I heard the news that we lost Dean some years later, he was a good man, gone too soon.

Then, I met John Starks. I liked talking to John Starks because the guy was down to earth. Starks had started at the bottom and worked his way to the top. He was a great basketball player. However, he was often overlooked at times. I was impressed with the way he kept his cool and focused on his game.

When I had the chance I shared with him my plans for the Worldwide Basketball Association. I told him about some of our programs and events. Starks asked questions about the events and gave me useful advice. One night he showed up at one of my events. It just happened to be my birthday, and I was having that event at a place called the Slate Lounge. I had made a lot of plans for that evening and wanted to invite a few of the former NBA players I had met. However, it was a cold February night and a lot of people decided not to show up. To my surprise, John Starks walked in the door with a huge smile on his face. It really made my night and showed me that we had made a connection. I then considered him a friend.

After his days playing basketball, John Starks was still a great role model, and he's the sort of person you want to work with. While I admire John for his efforts on the basketball court, I also admire him for the person he is off the court. John is still involved with Madison Square Garden in the front office, and he's always involved in events that help the community and assist young people with their plans for the future.

During a New York Knick celebration for the championship season, I had the opportunity to talk to another legend, Bernard King. Once again, I found a guy who was easy to talk to and very different from the persona that is projected by the media. Bernard struck me as a very sensitive guy and a deep thinker. He had great pride in himself. He believed in principles. I thought this was an important lesson. He also wrote a good book.

I think the WBA basketball programs really made a difference, even for the young girls who arrived. Crystal approached me at the end of that summer. She was a 17 year old from Harlem, and a runaway. Someone had signed her up for the camp, however, they did not pay. She showed up anyway, and we gave her a one-week pass for the camp. That experience of being in the camp inspired her to not only return home but to return to school.

I also had the pleasure of meeting some of the legendary ladies of professional basketball. I often took my daughter Maxine to Madison Square Garden to watch the New York Liberty make their run for the world championship.

I was so inspired by how these women conducted themselves as professional athletes, and I was well aware of the impression they could make on other young ladies. Sometimes it's overlooked that young girls love basketball too. So, I invited Kym Hampton to join our WBA camps for young ladies and conduct one of the motivational programs. Kym was a natural leader and ran one of the best camps.

That WBA program included tournaments and activities for young girls, and we even had co-ed games. My network continued to expand, and players like Teresa Weatherspoon expressed interest in our work and were great role models for the young girls.

I am still approached on the streets today by young men who participated in the WBA summer camps. Many confide that during those summers they were facing real challenges and that having the summer camp was a lifesaver. Some of these young men report that the summer camp helped them avoid prison. Alex was one of those teenagers at the camp, whose parents did not mail a check. He also was given a free pass. He told me that the camp motivated him to break away from a street gang that he was involved with. I had a great group of guys working with me at the WBA camps, guys like Shawn Grant, and my nephew Harold Lewis.

Another young man was now thirty-one years old and living on Roosevelt Island. Drew spoke to me one day. He thanked me for the WBA camp experience because he had been one of those young boys whose parents could not afford to pay. They dropped him off at the camp and forgot to bring a check. Yet, he reminded me of the words that scroll across the screen at the end of the movie *Schindler's List*: "Whoever saves one life, saves the world entire."

For the young people who attended the camps, it was a great experience. For many of the people who were employed by the WBA, it was a great opportunity. However, the WBA was not good for its investors, starting with its first investor, CEO Michael Williams. I did not recover my investment in the organization, nor did any of the other individuals who were part of a group of three men. It was a loss, and some relationships were never the same. But for all of the young people who attended the camps and benefited from the experiences, and for those who avoided jail during those summer camps, I say that I think it was worth the cost.

In the years that followed, I continued to follow Barnett. I watched as Dick Barnett, a former professional basketball player, transformed into Dr. Dick Barnett, educator, scholar, and author. He completed his doctoral degree at Fordham University and started teaching at St. John's University. Dr. Barnett also developed a new nonprofit organization to help disadvantaged groups in the community, and he has written about twenty books.

His transformation from a retired NBA basketball player to Ph.D. had a profound effect on me. Indeed, it sparked the beginning of my own journey into doctoral studies, and my effort to earn a Ph.D. First, I decided to pursue my master's degree.

There are some good things that a person can give to someone else; however, one of the best gifts of all is the gift of hope. I again remember Morgan Freeman's character in *The Shawshank Redemption.* In his reflection, Red says, "Hope is a dangerous thing." I think he was wrong. I think hope is the greatest gift that one person can give to the next. The man who took the time to buy me a cup of coffee on that day at Union Square gave me hope and motivated me to find a new life. My meeting with Barnett gave me hope that I could make a difference in other people's lives.

A CLASS ACT

Through my involvement with the WBA, I met another mentor and a good friend who provided critical lessons for me. To many, he's known as "Black Jesus" and "Black Magic." He was the original "Magic," a superstar before Magic Johnson.

I'm of course talking about Earl "The Pearl" Monroe. Monroe did everything with class and integrity, and I learned some important life lessons from him.

I sometimes flashback to when I was a young boy growing up in South Ozone Park. At that time the only thing that mattered to any young boy was the basketball league. For me, that was even more important than the pretty girls in the neighborhood.

The league was run by the Catholic Youth Organization or the CYO, and everybody in the neighborhood tried out for the team. I was still living at the group home, and none of the guys picked me to play in the schoolyard basketball games. So, it came as a shock when I was selected by the CYO league to play for the St. Theresa team. It was the one time that I was truly proud of myself.

The next most important thing for a young kid back then was the New York Knicks.

The Knicks were playing for the NBA championship in 1973. With their lineup that season, we believed that the Knicks were going to go all the way to the championship. The main reason that everyone was so excited was that the Knicks had brought over a player from Baltimore who we believed was the missing link to victory. We all called him Earl "The Pearl".

All the guys in the group home gathered around the TV to watch the New York Knicks make their run for the championship. We watched as Earl led the way.

During my time with the CYO basketball league, I even wore the number 15 jersey to honor Earl. I had a picture of his basketball card, and I signed his autograph myself because I knew I would never meet him. I would never have imagined that some twenty years later, through the WBA, Earl and I would become the best of friends.

The first time I met him, I was surprised that he actually had the time to talk, and was willing to give me advice about my plans to start the WBA nonprofit basketball league. Earl and I were both at a fundraiser to support Bill Bradley in his 1991 campaign for the President of the United States. The fundraiser was at the beautiful home of filmmaker Spike Lee, on 63rd Street and Lexington Avenue. Spike and his wife, Tanya, stood near the front and greeted each guest as they entered. All the basketball legends were in attendance. I had a chance to chat with Dave DeBusschere, and then Bill Bradley.

I had worked on a book with Dick Barnett that had allowed me to make use of my skills as an artist, and I was still able to draw fairly well. So, I asked Bradley and DeBusschere to sign a drawing of mine of a young man dunking a basketball. They signed a jersey for me, too.

Then I walked over to chat with Herb Williams, a member of the New York Knicks. Herb had decided to retire at the end of the year. While I was talking to Herb Williams, I looked up and noticed a man walking into the doorway. It was Earl Monroe! My head started to spin. I went up to introduced myself, and like most people, I started talking about my early years playing ball and being a big fan of the New York Knicks. Earl was very polite and even asked a few questions, like where had I grown up and what had my family been like. The conversion turned to business since at that time I was already thinking about a corporate sports league.

In that first meeting, Earl taught me an important lesson about integrity. I quickly realized that Earl hears a lot of pitches for new businesses, and while he likes to talk about new ideas and strategies, he also tests the person to see if they know what they are talking about. For example, he might say, "Tell me about your marketing plans. Is it all about marketing? That's why so many people have problems with a new business, they don't pay attention to the marketing plan."

I asked him, "How would you start this process if you were considering a new basketball league?"

Earl replied, "First and foremost, I want to know the people who are involved because I will not risk my name or reputation unless I am certain that everything is on point." He emphasized that his reputation and integrity were worth all the money in the world.

We continued to talk for a few more minutes. Then Spike Lee wanted to talk with Earl, so they walked away. I was proud of myself for not breaking down and asking for Earl's autograph.

My next meeting with Earl occurred about a year later when I was really starting to plan the WBA though it would still be a few years before we had the grand opening. Earl was always soft-spoken and genuinely concerned about real issues going on in the world. I had become accustomed to talking with people who were only concerned with making themselves a dollar.

I had watched so many men sell out, trade their good name for the money in a heartbeat. But Earl was not out to grab every dollar that he could get his hands on. I learned from Earl that your name was worth more than money. As the years started to go by, I found myself meeting with Earl more and more. I soon understood his views about integrity.

However, like Earl, I had my business concerns, about making a living and taking care of my family. He and I started meeting up to just talk about life and business. We sometimes met at Clyde's Wine and Dine on 10th Avenue. We would also meet at Earl's office for Reverse Spin Records, the music company he started after retiring from sports. My office for United Personnel Agency, Inc. had been on 42th Street and Madison Avenue. When we moved to 40th Street and Lexington, I was just a short walk from Earl's office.

In late 2015, I called Earl on the phone and he told me he had just moved into the new Reverse Spin Records office on West 39th Street. When I arrived at his office, he was unpacking his computer. His office was loft-style, and a few chairs, couches, and tables made the place feel very comfortable, like being in somebody's living room. On the walls, he had pictures of some of the NBA greats, like Kobe Bryant and Allen Iverson. To my surprise, Earl would assemble a desk by himself.

We also met a few times at the restaurant that he opened in Riverside Park, called "Earl Monroe". I really enjoyed meeting at the restaurant because I would always arrive early to get us a table. Nobody there knew me, so I didn't necessarily get the best table. Sometimes the waitress would pass by and just look at me.

Then Earl would walk into the restaurant and sit down with me. The place came alive! The manager would rush over to ask if we needed a better table, and the waitresses hustled to see if we needed anything. I would start laughing, and even Earl got the joke.

It was just plain fun hanging out with the legend. But one reason it was so much fun was that he didn't act like a legend. Earl is one of the only superstars I have ever met who does not have an ego. He had a very carefree approach to accepting life.

In 2006, movie director and lifelong Knicks fan Spike Lee produced "*He's Got Game*", which informed a whole new generation about Earl Monroe. Audiences soon realized that the movie was about "Black Jesus." Even my daughter, a millennial, heard of "Earl the Pearl." That movie informed people once again about a truly special guy.

But again, the real magic about Earl is his character, his sense of dignity, and his integrity. From Earl, I've learned important lessons about how to treat people, and how to treat yourself.

I also learned a lesson about friendship one Christmas. I was home alone that year. I would oftentimes visit with my daughters and grandkids on Staten Island or in Pennsylvania, but the past few years, both daughters had spent the holiday with their mother. So, I just stayed at home. I was still a bit of a loner in many ways and chose not to bother folks during the holiday.

Somehow, Earl became aware of this, and so he called me up and invited me to dinner at his home on 116th Street in Harlem. I accepted and was looking forward to having somewhere to go. I imagined that it would be quite a party, with maybe a few other former NBA players.

To my pleasant surprise, it was just me, Earl, his wife Marita, and their daughter Maya. Earl saw the surprised look on my face, and he said, smiling, "I was thinking of a nice, quiet, family dinner for Christmas."

Earl was telling me in a few words, *You are part of my family now.* I will always remember that holiday. We do our best to keep in touch. We talk about business or his visits to the doctor. Earl has had over forty operations. It is a miracle that he was able to endure that many operations. He just takes keeps moving on with his life.

Earl taught me some of the most important lessons about honesty, character, and integrity, and he did it with style. Most importantly, he taught me that my good name is priceless, a message that still resonates with me today. Earl taught me "Be yourself, and never sell out, your name is priceless". He helped me understand that your reputation was worth more than your weight in gold. Now, that is what I call real magic. However, I would learn that making changes to your character was a life-long pursuit.

CHAPTER 5

"No one can make you feel inferior without your consent."

Eleanor Roosevelt

THE SELF ESTEEM BLUEPRINT

It was the end of 2002, and I was finally able to experience a new level of success in my life. Yet, even before I could let it sink in, I made a critical mistake. It was the kind of mistake that would cost me the company I started in 1991, United Personnel Agency, Inc. I had decided to contract with a financial services company to provide funding. I did not realize that they could make a move to take the company from me. It was my struggle with ego and low self-esteem that set me up for the fall. I should have known by now. I learned that the first step on the road to making character changes concerns dealing with self-esteem. There were many signs of my struggle with self-esteem over the years.

For many years I had heard comments about my lack of eye contact. A small but important point. Yet, I hadn't connected this behavior to my low self-esteem and shame. But, during my early years as a destitute gambler, I had picked up the habit of walking hunched over. It was like I was looking for something on the ground, maybe lost money on the streets.

It shouldn't have surprised me that I was susceptible to falling into the trap of low self-esteem. Oddly, as a young boy, I had shown signs of having high self-esteem, even though I was living in an environment of extreme poverty and was growing up in a home with a single mother. I had this strange inner confidence that most young boys do not possess at that age. I think that my sense of self-esteem came from my mother's overabundance of love. Yes, we did struggle as a family, and we depended on the welfare system for subsistence. Yet, at that time I showed no signs of low self-esteem.

It wasn't until my first years at the Richmond Hill group home that my self-esteem started to decline. In the group home, life was about bullying, name-calling, physical abuse, and, of course, fighting. However, my sense of low self-esteem was more related to the feeling of having been abandoned. I had lost not only my mother but my entire family. I remember that no one came looking for me, that I received no visitors or phone calls.

I was simply forgotten. That feeling was exacerbated by my leaving the group home, my subsequent evictions, and my years living on the streets of New York City. Gambling offered an escape from my pain but losing money contributed to my sense of low self-worth.

My inner feelings were very self-demeaning. I was my worst critic. I was always anxious, frustrated, and depressed.

It was that books that got my attention early on. Some books were about the human body and how it works. These books showed how complex and mysterious the human body was. It was truly fascinating. What struck me most as I was reading was the fact that prominent men of science were still learning a lot about the machinery of the human body. Specifically, they seem to be mystified by the inner workings of the human brain. I noticed that when scientists tried to explain how the human brain functions, they often used words such as "phenomenon" or "miracle." I found it very puzzling that science could not explain the phenomenon of the brain, and that they considered the human body to be a miracle.

It occurred to me that if the human body was a miracle, then by implication I was also a miracle. That was the beginning of my journey of healing. I could feel a change within myself. I really began to see that every human life had value.

Now, I was looking people right in the eyes when I talked to them. I walked with my head up and a pep in my step. I greeted people with firm handshakes. Sometimes I even had a smile on my face.

Perhaps this was also the result of the time I had invested in working on myself in the support groups. It may have also been the result of having mentors like Dick Barnett, and Earl Monroe. All I knew was that something had changed within me. It was as if I had been touched by a powerful force that had healed my self-esteem and restored my soul. For the first time in my life, I felt like a man.

For the first time, I believed that I actually had a destiny. I woke up each morning and could feel my spirit soaring. When I looked at myself in the mirror, I finally liked what I saw. For the first time in my life, I felt good in my own skin.

I couldn't wait to get out and meet the challenges of each day. I felt so good about myself that I wanted to share the message of hope with the next person.

My support group had grown as well as my business network. By 2003, I made trips once a week to Wards Island, where I spoke to young people in the Odyssey House rehab program. The Odyssey House reminded me of Riker's Island, and the center's security officers in some ways resembled penitentiary correction officers. However, once I entered the large auditorium and saw the faces of the young men who had assembled for the discussion, I remembered my journey. I saw fear and confusion in those faces. I empathized. I understood how easily a young person could get lost.

My good friend Dennis T. who I knew from my support group, organized the discussions at Wards Island each week. He always thanked me heartily for joining him. He told me, "Mike, every time you talk to this group, I see the connection you're making. I hope you realize how much you touch the lives of these young men by telling your story."

I felt humbled and almost embarrassed. I replied, "Dennis, as much as I look forward to coming down here and working with these young men, believe me, I'm no saint! My reasons are also selfish—I want to remember my journey. I understand what these young men are going through. I can still feel the pain myself. I do not want to forget, so I come here."

Most times I spoke to the groups without a microphone. I usually started my talk by describing my difficult days living at the group home, then transitioned to my time on the streets looking for a place to sleep. Then, I shared the moment that I knew it was time to make some changes, what I call "resurrection time: I talked a lot about denial because I know what a powerful obstacle can be when a person is trying to find a new direction in life. Finally, I talked about adjusting to the world that I live in today, where I have responsibility and opportunity.

After speaking, when I looked at the faces of the men in the audience, I would see a little light in some of their eyes. I could tell when I had made a connection because that person's eyes would fix directly on mine.

One of the young men, Gabe, walked up to me after the break. He said, "Mr. Williams, thank you for coming to talk to us today. Your words were really powerful for me, especially the part that you shared about dealing with low self-esteem, self-doubt, and self-hate. That's me."

He continued, "I've been doing a lot of negative things to myself and the people around me. But listening to you today, I know I must make some changes." I maintained eye contact with him as he spoke. That was very important.

I was again humbled, and I told him, "Gabe, I'm really happy you are here today. Life is about transformation, and we are all either going in one direction or the other. We are either getting better or getting worse. There is no in-between. So, think about how you use your time and energy. The important thing to take away from this is that the time to act is now because time is not your friend. Let's keep talking and let's keep in touch."

Once I made that connection with a person, I would feel a boost of energy and excitement. Once I knew that I had their attention, I could hope that their life would change in the next moment. Having a cup of coffee with that stranger so many years ago was my "resurrection time" In some way, I felt I had to repay that debt by continuing to carry the message of hope to others.

I volunteered with other nonprofit organizations whose missions were to help disadvantaged families. One of the organizations I worked with was called Downey Side, a nonprofit that locates permanent families for older kids in foster care. I had the opportunity to work with homeless teenage boys who struggled with the same type of depression, anxiety, and low self-esteem I had experienced myself. The experience always served as a reminder to me.

I did my best to encourage them to believe in themselves. I wanted to see these boys make it in life. I tried to stay in touch with them over the years. There were a few experiences that made me very angry because they were clear reminders that people take advantage of the vulnerable.

At Downey Side, I met a young man in the program, named Corey, who had some learning disabilities and mental illness. Corey was about twenty years old and had dropped out of high school. He had finally decided to move out of Downey Side to try living on his own. To prepare for being on his own again, he had saved up some money. When I spoke to Corey on the phone, I didn't like the sound of the arrangement he had made with a lodger.

He first talked about finding a room, which sounded okay. He then told me that it was not a single room and that he would be sharing the bed with the current tenant of the apartment. Corey told me that the tenant had suggested that they bunk together for a while. My response was "COREY, HELL NO!"

I believed that because of his mental illness, Corey did not understand the situation he was getting himself into. I imagined that the so-called tenant, whoever he was, was a sicko trying to take advantage of this young man. So, I told Corey to forget about the arrangement and not even try to get his money back. I provided him with some money, then I made some phone calls and I provided him with directions to a new place that could provide a single room.

I always felt that more was needed to help these nonprofits and the young men in them. I believed that I was making a positive contribution to the community. I still needed to keep my ego in check. I was making fast decisions, and it seemed that some were quite costly. I needed to watch my steps, particularly, in business, and my private life.

It seemed that some days my old demons tapped me on the shoulder and reminded me that they were still around. That was one of the challenges of recovery: I had to always guard against a relapse. A few men in my support group had told me that this addiction does not give up but just keeps coming at you. When I'm in the room with my group listening to therapy and getting support, my disease is in the hallway doing push-ups.

Indeed, I had finally experienced some real success in my life, and I had resources available. Ironically, that was the challenge. I still struggled with my ego and the "big shot syndrome." Despite my success, I still had some important lessons to learn.

I had to learn more about "triggers". That means, people, places, and things can all be triggers that set a person back on the wrong path and let the demons out of their cages. This is why my recovery group was so important. I had to learn about "triggers". This can be the loss of a job, the loss of a relationship, the death of a family member or friend, or something as simple as rejection. I needed to identify my own triggers and keep them in check. My decision to contract with a financial services company to fund my payroll was a trigger. It was as if I subconsciously wanted to fail. In some ways, I set a trap for myself. It goes back to the struggle with self-esteem, and self-sabotage.

I also still had to be aware of denial. When I saw ads for Las Vegas on the television, I still really wanted to believe that I could visit the place just one time and gamble like a normal person. Yet, I knew it would be a big mistake to give in to these urges now. This time, I reminded myself, I would be hurting my family as well as myself.

If I wanted to protect my recovery, I needed to do more. I was also looking out for my family. My daughter Maxine lived with me now. If I fell down again, this time I would hurt the people I love. I needed to try harder, and do more for my recovery. So I would call one of my group members for support.

For example, Big Mike had over thirty years of sobriety and was somebody that I could always count on. One day though, I received the shocking news that Big Mike had returned to gambling. I could not believe that after thirty-three years in the program, he gave in to his disease. The news turned everything upside down. Now, I was really thinking about a trip to Atlantic City. I dreamed about the lights and glamour of the casinos.

So I called another member and left him a message. I got a callback, this time about Mark, another group member that I was very close to and depended on. More bad news: Mark had also returned to gambling. Worse, Mark was an attorney and had embezzled money from his clients. By the time I got the phone call, he was already in jail.

Mark's wife and three kids were devastated. I was trying to figure out what was going on. As hard as I tried to stay on the right track, my disease was calling to me, and I heard it loud and clear. It was not a good week. I still had to resolve the problem with the finance company that was funding my payroll. It was time to buckle down and try to ride it out. I decided to reach out to my recovery group again.

Within a month, some of the strongest members in my support group fell. I saw this as a call to take self-inventory and to do some soul-searching. I was wrestling with the meaning of these relapses, of all those years of struggle and the commitment to recovery. Of all the meetings and the weekend retreats. Of all the years of trying to carry a message of hope. The years of believing that every experience has a message. What did they mean?

I began to question everything. What was my message? I was learning about transformation, determination, redemption, and self-improvement. But, I needed to dig deeper. Fortunately, all my years of hard work with the support group paid off. The work I did to improve my self-esteem was beginning to show. It was time for me to think like a leader.

My group members would now turn to me for support. It was time to step up. I felt that I had something valuable to share with my group members. Specifically, I hoped to share how I had used the power of positive thinking to change the direction of my life. I wanted to share my experience with others.

I call this my "self-esteem blueprint", a vision of where I want to be and how to avoid the "self-sabotage traps". I had set a trap that could cost me my business, or my recovery. I needed to learn why, and how to address that situation. But it was a very challenging process. At times I found it quite difficult to avoid the traps, especially the traps that involved the people within my inner circle. However, I made a rather revealing connection between the circumstances and the traps that I sometimes walked into.

THE SELF-SABOTAGE TRAP

By 2003, it seemed that I was still living a double life. I was experiencing some real success in business, and yet, I was living each day on the edge. It seemed that every decision was important. However, my judgment was not always up to the task. I made a very important decision, and I overlooked some key factors.

I starting working with a finance company that provided my staffing agency with lines of credit and funding services. What I didn't know was that many of these finance companies used certain strategies to take control of other companies, particularly companies owned by people of color. They knew that the economy was changing and that credit would become the most critical factor for a small business.

While working with this company, I let my guard down. I was depending more and more on the lines of credit to fund my payroll. Once again, I was setting myself up to fall. This time I set my own trap. I used the lines of credit to run my business. Then, this company canceled the line of credit. They knew my clients took sixty or ninety days to pay their fees, and I only had funds for my payroll for thirty days. The finance company was trying to use this as a justification for taking control of my company.

During this time I had to use all of the principles and knowledge that I had learned about motivation and determination. This was also a test of my recovery as a compulsive gambler because financial pressure was one of my main triggers. I did not want to lose my company.

I arranged a meeting with a senior manager from the finance company. This individual was confident I would sign the company over to the finance company. He tried to mislead me at first, and I pretended to be naïve. But, I had no intention of selling out. He arrived at 9 AM sharp.

I said, "Good morning, Mr. Kater, I appreciate you taking the time to see me today. I understand we have a serious problem here: after thirty days, I will not have the funds to pay my employees, which means I am out of business. I understand your company is canceling my line of credit because you're concerned about my clients paying their invoices, and our payment schedules"

I continued, "I'm trying to find a way forward, and I find some of the conditions you're imposing to be quite unfair."

Mr. Kater stared out the window as I talked. Then he said, "Yes, Mr. Williams, we have seen this happen quite often, especially under present conditions, and I can assure you that if we do some type of merger with your company, you will still have a job—you'll just be working directly for us."

I did my best not to show my anger. It had taken me sixteen years to build this company and I didn't do it to just end up working for another company. However, I also knew that I had failed to plan for a rainy day. I could have set-up a reserve payroll account. I was too busy taking vacations, and playing the role of the "bigshot".

So I replied, "I understand your reasoning for cutting off our line of credit, but I still have some big problems with what you are doing. You have my accounts receivable, my client list, and you know that my clients include Merrill Lynch, Bank of America, Wells Fargo, and Bank of New York…These are not the type of clients that you need to be concerned about paying the agency invoices"

Mr. Kater shifted in his chair.

I continued, "Yes, some clients are paying slowly right now, I understand that. But why are you cutting off my credit? You're essentially forcing me to give up my company."

At first, he didn't speak. Finally, he said, "Mr. Williams, I understand what you're saying. However, your clients have a lot of money outstanding right now. We just cannot extend any more credit to your company, and we know it is going to take sixty days or more for these clients to pay you. You only have enough in your account to last thirty days."

Mr. Kater concluded, "You must make a decision. I know it doesn't seem this way to you, but we're here to help you. Like I told you, after all, is said and done, you will still have a job. I hope you call me later so we can get the process going."

And with that, he walked out of my office. I stood looking out the window for a long time. I knew the real reason behind all this was race.

Mr. Kater had a problem with working with a black man as the owner of the company. What he saw was a black man who was not accountable to anyone, who was making his own decisions independently. As far as he was concerned, there was something wrong with that picture.

This merger plan was a way for him to resolve that problem. His company would take control of my agency, and then I would work for him.

I was proud of myself for not showing my anger, but I knew quite well I was not giving up my company. For the next thirty days, I continued to work knowing full well I would run out of funds at the end of the month, and that I would risk my payroll checks bouncing. In the staffing business, if you bounce a payroll check; Game over. Once the word is out on the street, your company is done.

I had a few sleepless nights. I did try to remember all that I had learned from the books I had read. Once again, I was depending on everything I had learned about positive thinking, and even my old premise in my days as a gambler, "If you pray for rain, bring an umbrella." As the end of the month approached, and I was just a few days away from running out of funds, I started thinking outside of the box.

Then inspiration struck. I picked up the phone and called my old friend and accountant Phil Baumgarten. He was the guy who was able to get me started in the business. However, he only did my tax returns now. Phil did not know about my financial struggles with the finance company. So, we had a meeting. What happened next caught me off guard. We discussed my problem and came up with a plan to open a new business, our own payroll company, called United Payroll Systems, Inc. Phil was once again able to find the investors because he did everyone's taxes and he knew who did and did not have money. One of the investors would be CEO, and Phil would be the CFO. I was able to end my contract with the other financial company and continue operating United Personnel Agency. It was a close call. It was time to face the music. It was time to learn the lessons of self-sabotage. I could not just blame racism for the situation that nearly cost me my company.

The self-sabotage trap is a mental state, the place in my mind and in my heart where I allow procrastination, fear, and a lack of faith to take hold. The self-sabotage trap is the place in my head where other people's opinions rent space for free. In that place, my demons live for a chance to re-emerge- especially the one I call "the Ghost of If Only."

The "Ghost of If Only" has done more to sabotage my dreams than any other demon. It is a haunting echo in the back of my mind that says, "*If only* I had more money, *if only* I had important friends, *if only* I had a second chance, *if only* I were younger *if only* I had someone to support me!"

"*If only* I were not so fat! *If only* I was not so stressed out, *if only* I had a better boss, *if only* I had a better job *if only* I didn't have a past, *if only* I had a good education, *if only* other people liked me, *if only* I could like myself."

But as William Shakespeare said, "To thine own self be true." His words have great meaning for me. To confront the self-sabotage trap, it was necessary for me to be true to myself. I was responsible for laying the groundwork for the "self-sabotage trap".

I remembered the words of Eleanor Roosevelt that "No one can make you feel inferior without your consent.". I was the one who was to decide.

I have been able to tackle self-sabotage at different times, I had help from my recovery groups, it was always a step-by-step process. Yet, self-improvement is a lifelong commitment, so I would still experience times when I might walk into the next trap.

In late 2004 I received a phone call from Mr. Morris, my account manager at Chase Bank. There was a serious problem with my payroll account. Mr. Morris said to me, "Mr. Williams, one of your clients gave you a check that has been returned due to lack of funds. Now your payroll checks are not covered."

I could hear the tension in his voice. I reassured him that I would handle the matter. Even large clients make mistakes. "Mr. Morris, I am already in touch with that client and will be at your office this morning with a deposit."

By this time I was growing fatigued from running my own business. I had expanded my office in midtown Manhattan and was now operating two corporations, United Personnel Agency and Worldwide Basketball Association at the same time. My office space was midsize but cozy. There were the portraits on the walls of Martin Luther King, Jr., and President John F. Kennedy. There was also a portrait of the jazz musician Dexter Gordon, which I put up after seeing him in the movie *Round Midnight.* On any given day, after my secretary Charlotte greeted you, you could find me at my desk. I was working seven days a week and it was not unusual for me to work one hundred hours a week. When I took time off, my secretary Charlotte, became CEO. She ran the company for me. Which caused her to have a lot of sleepless nights. However, after operating United Personnel Agency for sixteen years, change was bound to come. The problem with Chase Bank was a red flag.

I also felt strongly that my responsibility as a father had to take priority over my business. At first, I had worked out an arrangement with my ex-wife to have my children on weekends. Then, some years after my divorce, my younger daughter Maxine told her mother that she wanted to live with her father. This was a big decision for a 12-year-old girl, and, oddly, she was the same age as I had been when I lost my mother. I knew immediately that I would have a tremendous challenge in operating my own company and being a full-time parent.

On one hand, I understood that the image of me operating United Personnel Agency made a powerful impression on my daughter. A few years later, Maxine graduated high school as an honor student. She was offered a four-year scholarship to one of the top schools in Rhode Island and became a CPA, starting her career working for Bank of America. She soon got married and my granddaughter and grandson were born. But, I am thankful that growing up she experienced a father who was both a business owner and a dad.

My oldest daughter Juleah was proud of me as a business owner and understood what that means. One summer after she came home from college, she even decided to work for my company. Juleah is now thirty-five years old and the mother of two great kids and I believe that she knows in her heart that I did my all to be the best dad that I could be.

I also loved being CEO and President of United Personnel Agency, thereby providing jobs to thousands of people, mostly low-income and minority individuals.

Yet I knew it would be difficult to continue to balance being a business owner and a single father. I knew it was time to make a change. That morning when the bank manager called was just another big red flag. I had spent too many mornings putting out fires. And, despite my best efforts, I had not effectively managed United Personnel Agency, as well as I should have. The company was in trouble again. So, it was time to act. This time I was ready to do a merger.

Fortunately, I had already been approached by a large staffing agency based out of Melville, in Long Island. They wanted to do a buyout. They were interested in buying my company. Furthermore, this agency had offered me the position of VP, so I could continue working with my clients and providing services to the community. I had my reservations about letting go of my company. I questioned whether it was a sign of failure.

Deep down inside I did not feel like a failure. It was just time to make a change. However, I could at least do this on my own terms, and it was not the result of a hostile takeover, such as what almost took place the year before. This time I had a choice.

This was not a takeover, it was an offer to buy my company. My mind began to race. How much would they offer to buy my company? I dreamed of a million-dollar buyout. Yet, I resisted giving up control of the company. Then, I thought about my daughter Maxine, who was now living with me. I knew that I could not have it all. It was time to let go of the company. I was quite intrigued about what the buyout price would be for the company.

So I called the staffing agency, and I agreed to sell United Personnel Agency. We scheduled the meeting for the following Monday. During the merger, I struggled with my ego and my sense of self-worth, but I finally understood. I knew it was not a question of failure or success. It was simply time to make a decision. As before in my life, I believed I would find a way forward. Yet the ego can still get in the way of progress.

THE BIG SHOT SYNDROME

The financial crisis that hit the U.S. economy in 2007 actually hit employment agencies two years earlier. I had made the mistake of matching my sense of self-worth to the success of my business. When I had to sell the company and do the merger, I struggled with the idea that the merger was a sign of my failure as a business owner. To add to the challenges at that time, the economy became unstable in other sectors as well.

For a long time I believed that if I was doing well in my business, it meant that I was a good person. So by selling and closing my company, I found myself in a tug-of-war with my self-esteem and my ego. I often would talk with someone in my support group to get some perspective. My good friend Dave, who operated his own real estate company, was my go-to person.

Dave was a humble guy and very down-to-earth. He was based in Manhattan and had over a hundred brokers working for him. Dave had a nice office. I liked the large windows, which allowed in a lot of sunlight. The atmosphere was bustling with people moving through the office, everyone trying to make a real estate deal. But for a guy running such a big company, Dave was very soft-spoken and easy-going. He was also recovering from an alcohol and gambling addiction.

I got in touch with him to talk about the circumstances of the merger. I told him that I was feeling a lot of inner turmoil about myself as a person and as a business owner. "I do this all the time. If things are not going well for me in business, I start telling myself that I am not a good person. The worst part is, this can be a trigger, and I start thinking about Atlantic City."

Dave looked into my eyes when I mentioned Atlantic City. He didn't speak but merely nodded his head. He stared at a picture of a lighthouse hanging on the wall. Then his eyes flickered back to me.

I continued, "I still fantasize about the dream world, about the women and the champagne, even though I know it would all lead me back to the gutter. Dave, I don't get the connection between the merger and this fantasy about Atlantic City."

Dave listened carefully. Then he said, "Sure, we both know about triggers, and we know why they come when they do. If you are feeling a little low it's an opportunity for your disease to talk to you. It sounds like you want to get rid of the pain, and you want to get rid of the fear, which means you want to run away. But we both know that leads nowhere. You can't just escape. Like I just told another guy, who was saying something similar to you, it doesn't matter where you go, because you have to take yourself along."

I listened to Dave and his words resonated like a bell. He was reminding me that self-improvement is a lifelong process. My challenge was to avoid allowing my feeling about the merger to dictate my sense of self-worth, or become a trigger for a trip to Atlantic City. When I left the office, I thought about what Dave had told me. It was time to make a move.

It took about three days to complete the arrangements for the merger, including the buyout. I was still dreaming about a million-dollar buyout. The Melville agency made an interesting offer but, I was disappointed. They had learned about my situation and knew that I needed to sell. They knew the recession would be ugly. I thought about my daughter and the battles facing me. My mother told me "Be careful how you pick your battles" So, we did the deal. I then merged my office with a new company. I gave the check for the buyout to Mr. Morris at Chase Bank. My accounts were all on overdraft. "Mr. Morris, please deposit this check into my accounts, and close everything out. I sold the company today, please transfer the balance into my personal account" Mr. Morris seemed a bit shocked, and yet relieved. He knew that I did not want to give up my company, and had fought for years to hold on. Now the battle with my ego was over. For now. I thanked him for his help during those years.

Most people do not know how important it is to have a relationship with your banker. I did my best to make the company work for sixteen years. But now it was over, and time to move on. I would still have a good sum of money in my checking account after he settled my payroll and operating account. For a moment, I thought about a trip to Las Vegas. It was a place that I had never had the chance to visit. Instead, I walked over to Lexington Ave, to see my new office. Now, I accepted my new role as Vice President of Marketing with the Melville agency.

My main focus was now developing my client base and finding new clients.

The first week, I really struggled, I was having flashbacks. One habit that persisted was that I still found myself involved in relationships of little substance. I often found myself back at some strip club talking to a dancer. I believe this tendency was rooted in a part of me that still wanted a quick and easy way to enjoy life. It seemed that the old gambler was still kicking around in the back of my mind. I had just sold my business and needed to do something, go somewhere. For some reason, it seemed that I was still in a big hurry to go nowhere. So I did not need to take the time to build real relationships. In my mind, it was much easier to meet a lady in a nightclub and invite her to go away with me on a weekend cruise. When these flings did not work out, I found myself struggling with that same feeling of low self-esteem and shame.

This may sound strange to a lot of people. However, it was textbook behavior for a compulsive gambler. I think I spent many years as what we call a "dry drunk." I was no longer gambling, but I was still a gambler at heart.

For example, one evening in a nightclub, I invited a very attractive lady to join me for a cruise. She worked in the coat check room. I told her to go home after work and pack her suitcase, and then meet me at the airport. I may have had a few too many drinks. Yet, to prove to her that I wasn't just talking, I took off my gold-and-diamond college graduation ring and gave it to her. I told her to hold onto the ring until we met the next day at the airport, where she could return it to me. If I was not at the airport when she arrived, I promised, she could keep the ring, which was worth $500. I told her she could sell it.

Guess what! I never saw that young lady again. I felt pretty stupid for losing my ring. Then something even odder happened. I returned to the bar and was approached by another woman, she was the bartender. She told me that she was the roommate of the lady that I had waited for at the airport. The roommate was aware that I had given the woman my ring, and she knew that her friend was leaving town that week. So the roommate told me, she had stolen the ring back to return it to me.

I was surprised, to say the least. The roommate was very nice, not as attractive as her friend, but she had my ring. I thanked her for returning it to me, and I gave her a few hundred dollars as a reward. Of course, in the back of my mind, I couldn't help but wonder if the two women were working together and if the whole thing was a scam. I can only tell you that this experience did very little to help my battle with low self-esteem.

What did help was my recovery group and learning more about how to build up my self-esteem. I had to admit to my group this dumb mistake. It was important for me to continue to take my self-inventory and face tough questions like, why did I still have such a low opinion of myself?

I started to become more aware of the people around me and how I handled my relationships. I especially became more careful about the people I interacted with. I became aware of what I call "energy vampires." These are people who try to feed on other peoples' positive energy. These are the folks who told me that I would never succeed in the employment business in the middle of a recession. These were the folks who questioned my goal of returning to school.

To handle these negative experiences, I actually became a bit of a loner. I looked inward for answers. I took inventory of my life and put all my goals into writing so I could see them each day. I made a list of the positive things in my life and my meaningful accomplishments. I repeated this list to myself every morning. I also reminded myself of what I had learned about the miracle of the human body. I reminded myself that I was also a miracle. I reminded myself to be aware of the driving forces of ego, power, and sex.

It was time for me to accept the fact that my affairs with women in night clubs or strip clubs were not contributing to healthy self-esteem, and were damaging my recovery. I needed to find more meaningful relationships. It was time to meet women who wanted to go to dinner and take a walk in the park. Yet I still struggled with the personality of the compulsive gambler. Inside, I still wanted to just buy a woman a drink, tell a few jokes, and then take a cab back to my place. I still wanted the dream world and I thought because I no longer gambled, it would be different.

I also realized that as I confronted my fears and addressed my behavior, I finally found ways to stop wasting money. In simple terms, the less money I wasted, the better I felt about myself. Once I began to see some progress, I became much more hopeful.

I also became more introverted and began to be aware of the people around me. As my self-esteem grew, I reduced the number of people around me. I became more isolated and conservative in some ways.

I continue to keep to myself even today, and I still watch out for "energy vampires." I keep myself busy. I believe the saying that an "idle mind is the devil's workshop." What makes the process so compelling is that even after I reach one plateau, I'm aware that my battle for self-esteem was far from over.

Building self-esteem is a lifelong pursuit. It is a step-by-step process and there is no graduation date. It is also important to look out for signs that could trigger a setback.

However, we had made history. The United States elected a new president, and for the first time, he was a black man. The election of Barack Obama was monumental for men like me. We all felt more pride the next day, and we walked with a spring in our step. However, the looming financial devastation would cast a dark shadow on that shining moment.

I also decided to close the Worldwide Basketball Association. The WBA was more show than tell, a lot more about ego than good works. For example, during the early stages of the WBA, I decided we would focus on the community and youth programs. I would operate the programs for adults separately. I planned to throw an event in the fall of that year to create some interest in the community.

Once again, I went over the top in my planning. We had newspaper articles written about the event and I reached out to Dick Barnett, Earl Monroe, Walt Frazier, Charles Smith, and John Starks to invite them to the event. I reserved a large reception hall for the event and invited over three hundred people. There was an open bar, and the food was great. It was just what my ego needed. I was the center of attention.

I had pictures taken with me standing front and center, with all the NBA legends standing behind me. So, there I was, dressed in my white tux, big smile. I saw this as my time to let the world know who was in charge, call me "Mr. Big Shot".

I was not even managing the front door to the event correctly. I should have had someone collect tickets. I was foolish enough to use the honor system and allowed the people coming in to be seated before collecting their tickets. This was the big shot syndrome on steroids. But true to code, when the affair was over, the bar bill was left unpaid. Many of the guests who attended the event had not even paid for their tickets.

They probably figured, why should I pay for this event? Let "Mr. Big Shot" handle it. He acts like he has a million bucks. There was a song once, called "Mr. Big Stuff". I could hear the lyrics playing in my head. *Mr. Big Stuff, Who do you think you are, You think you're higher than every star above.* There is nothing like an overinflated ego, to bring down a business.

I tried to keep the WBA going for as long as possible, but soon after that event, I had to shut the organization down due to a lack of resources and funding. We did not even get support from the community. Some of the corporations who had signed on didn't pay for their sponsorship. I was not surprised, because the recession had caused some real damage to many companies and organizations.

However, I had to inform all my investors that they would likely take a loss on the WBA. This was a blow not only to my ego but to my pocket as well, I had made a significant investment of my own. And, also because most of the investors were my good friends, like Phil Baumgarten and Andy Goold. Phil had been with me from the very beginning, first as my accountant and then as the person who organized the first two investment groups that helped me start my businesses. I had convinced him to join two other investors in putting their money into the WBA. Andy had hired me as a young sales representative in my early years in the staffing business. I invited them in as investors. Yet, I saw signs of trouble from the very beginning. I went forward anyway. I made the mistake of not going back and doing some due diligence. It was another sign that my ego was out of touch with reality.

Dealing with my ego was a unique challenge because sometimes I was right about my decisions and sometimes I was wrong. It was like the old gambler's mentality. For all the times that I was right, my ego would soar. For every time I was wrong, my ego preferred denial. Ultimately, despite all the work I had done in my recovery groups, and even on my spiritual retreat weekends, I still struggled with the need to impress people and win approval.

One of my friends from the support groups has an interesting definition of ego. Bernie explained to me, the word **EGO** stands for *Easing God Out.* When the EGO takes over, a person thinks that they are the center of the universe.

I must admit I was surprised to find myself struggling with my ego at this stage of my life. I did work on my recovery. The first step is all about being humble and grateful. But it was clear that there was a still battle within me. Part of that battle was with my ego and concerned my inability to face reality, even as a person who no longer gambled.

For example, back in 2003, when my daughter Maxine decided to move to New York to live with me, I was still doing my big shot bit and she did not have any idea of any difficulties ahead. Yet by 2006, I had a problem paying for her college education. Even at the very end, when she was packing to leave for school, I still could not tell her about my financial situation. Why? Because of my ego.

Later, Maxine was in quite a bit of shock when she realized just how ill-prepared I was for her going to college. She remembered me as a man with all the answers. I was her dad and the one she could count on. She watched me take groups of people on cruises. I would take out a credit card and pay for the whole vacation. I even allowed her to invite her friends from school, and I would pay for everything. So she could not understand how I was not prepared to pay for her college education.

I finally had to tell my daughter that I had planned poorly. Combined with the economic crisis, that meant there were many things I could no longer do. I was very fortunate that she had done so well in school and received a four-year scholarship to Bryant University in Rhode Island.

I often wondered why I still struggled with the big shot syndrome. Then I realized that "the big shot syndrome" was my response to my low self-esteem. The big shot syndrome is all about perception and how a person wants to be perceived by people around him.

In other words, to compensate for my sense of low self-esteem, I needed others to see me in a different light. The big-shot syndrome traces back to the start of my gambling addiction and my desire to be needed and wanted. I would do anything to maintain the image that I wanted other people to see.

The big shot syndrome doesn't just afflict the guy with the white-collar job at the big financial company. It can influence the grandmother who takes that weekly bus trip to Atlantic City so that she can overspend on her grandkids and earn their love. The big shot syndrome can affect a young mother who wants to spoil her first child. The big shot syndrome can affect anybody who wants to feel important. What really added to my situation was that I had never had money, and then I quickly found myself with resources at my disposal.

I always remind myself of those years as a homeless man sleeping on the streets. It is always best to not forget the journey. To remember the past. I decided to go back to basics and do the things that had allowed me to make progress in the very beginning. I decided to attend more meetings each week and make at least two or three phone calls to other group members every week. It was also time to get back to the weekend recovery retreats. Recovery is a life-long work in progress. I finally met a lady at a black-tie party. Monique was twenty years younger than me but very mature. She looked a little bit like Mary J. Blige. We just hit it off really well. The year just flew by. There was never any pressure about marriage, or even moving in together. Somehow the relationship held together. I decided if it's not broken, then leave it alone. I still had other issues to deal with.

Many people who don't struggle with addiction think that at some point, an addict "graduates" to being a non-addict. But that's not true. We never stop learning, never stop having to check our ego and our intentions. Recovery is a lifelong, one-day-at-a-time process. Only when you have been dead for three days can they can mark your headstone "Cured."

CHAPTER 6

"...No, he's a gambler." Gatsby hesitated, then added: "He's the man who fixed the World Series back in 1919."

F. Scott Fitzgerald, The Great Gatsby

LIVING WITH OBSESSION

I'd been living in a world without gambling for almost twenty-five years. I had been living on Roosevelt Island for more than ten years, and I still smile when I looked out my front window at the East River. I feel like I became a winner by not gambling.

The last few years had been bumpy, but I finally learned to put my ego in my back pocket. I settled into my new role as VP of Marketing with the staffing agency. I now spent my days taking clients out to lunch and dinner. I didn't know what a bad day was anymore. I just felt extremely grateful for what my life was.

I woke up each morning and looked in my closet to pick out a suit. I went downstairs to the café and enjoyed a wonderful breakfast. Then I took the subway train one stop and I arrived at 63rd and Lexington Avenue in midtown Manhattan. My office was ten minutes away. I just had to walk out my door and embrace life.

However, in many ways, I was still that man who used to wake up in the subway with rats crawling all over him. I was still restless, and despite everything, I still had an obsessive-compulsive personality. By the end of 2009, the financial crisis had devastated the economy, even my own company. I was losing my clients and business was slowing down. So, it didn't take long before the wheels started turning again, and I was thinking of my next move.

The world was changing. The new president, Barack Obama, was showing us a different style of leadership. He was taking on some real challenges because the economy was going from bad to worse. The U.S. experienced the loss of 800,000 jobs in one month. Yet, we witness Sonia Sotomayor become the first Hispanic woman to serve on the U.S. supreme court. Then, a miracle, Chesley Sullenberger landed his plane in the Hudson River, saving the lives of every person on that flight.

I managed to have a productive start to my first full year as a student in the master's program. I was still involved in the community and sometimes would visit the same nonprofit organizations where I met many of the homeless men who lived at the Bowery Men's Shelter. It was always a good reminder for me to visit these men.

Then, I heard the sad news that Michael Jackson had died. We were the same age, 50 years old. I remember growing up in South Ozone Park Queens, and the young girls thinking that I was him. It was difficult to wrap my mind around the idea that he was dead. I turned on the radio. A song was playing "Pretty Young Thing". It still sounded good. I still struggle when I think he is dead. However, there was a message in his death for me to acknowledge. We all have our demons to face and try to defeat. It seems that Michael did not prevail in his battle with his demons.

I still had my battles from time to time, and because of my recovery group, I was learning how to confront my demons. I was also learning to live with a condition that some call obsessive behavior. I was still finding ways to re-direct or re-channel my focus and energy. However, because of the economic crisis, my concerns were about making a living.

I was thinking it was time to start a new business. I also realized that it was time to talk to a professional therapist about my obsessive-compulsive behavior. I was given the name of a lady, Dr. Wagner. She was a white lady, mid-forties, and very soft-spoken. Her office was located on 73rd Street and Riverside Drive. I began to meet with her once a week. She agreed to a sliding scale for her fee after I explained some of the financial pressures that I was currently dealing with. The sessions with Dr. Wagner became part of a "historic breakthrough" in my recovery and personal life. She often put some difficult questions to me. "Why do you think that the threat of returning to gambling is so strong in your life now?" I replied, "I sometimes think I used that as a way to cope, it became my outlet, my great escape, even though I know where it all leads".

She replied "What about your family? You have searched for many years to find your family, how did you maintain your motivation? I replied "I was driven by the need to feel whole, and I was motivated by anger and fear. I was afraid that my younger brother and sister would meet one day, and not know they were related, I had nightmares about that, I felt guilty too, like any young boy, you get angry at your mother, and you say bad things, I was so angry that I did not give my mom a kiss goodnight, I was still upset that morning when I left for school.

Later that day she died. I hated myself for being angry at her, and for not kissing her goodbye. I never had the chance to say "sorry mom".

So, now I see that my meetings with Dr. Wagner were making a difference. I started to really learn how to deal with my emotions and depression. I was also beginning to learn how to deal with my obsessive-compulsive behavior. I started to feel empowered.

Though I think that I've channeled my obsessive-compulsive energies into some positive outlets, it was still something that required real work.

I was also learning to live with what I called my "OCD tendencies" I am sure this condition can be very frustrating for most people. It means experiences with excessive actions, reoccurring thoughts, and compulsions. For example, if I heard a line from a song that I liked, I repeated the lyrics to myself hundreds of times that day. I would replay an event that happened over and over in my mind. I could read the same book six or seven times in a row and not lose focus. I could go to the same theater and watch the same movie eight or nine times. I would tell myself, I'm going to see something in the movie that I missed the first seven watches. I have seen the movie *Casablanca* over one hundred times. I now have it memorized.

So for a long time, my obsessive-compulsive behavior was a liability. I could have wasted my entire life consumed by my drive to gamble. Fortunately, I found ways to turn it into an asset. For example, when I found my first books on motivation and self-help, I read the same book thirty times until I had memorized whole pages.

I told her about a very profound experience as a 19-year-old. This experience shows how fragile life is. It is a memory that haunts me to this day. I had enrolled in a class at John Jay College of Criminal Justice. I wanted to complete my undergrad degree, and then go on to law school. However, those early years were very difficult. Even when I did get a student loan check, I wasted the money at the racetrack.

I was on my way to class and did not have the money to pay my subway fare. So that I would not miss my train, I jumped over the turnstile and began running. I was carrying my briefcase, which contained, among other things, my books.

As soon as I jumped over the turnstile, I heard a voice yell, "Hey, you! Stop! Pay your fare! Hey, I said stop!"

Instead, I panicked and ran faster. The voice said, "For the last time, you better stop right now! Put your hands up!"

That made me freeze. I slowly turned to see a police officer standing right behind me. He was a young black man, dressed in his blue uniform. He was out of breath, and with one hand was pointing a finger at me. With the other, he held his gun.

He said, "Dammit, you did you not hear me? Did you not hear me say freeze? I was ready to put a bullet in your back."

I noticed that this officer was not more than thirty years old. I replied, "Thank you for not putting a bullet in my back." I had a quick flashback. I was thinking of my brother Richard and imagined how crazy it was that I almost got shot running from a cop to get to my class. So I stopped running. We were both out of breath. I saw sweat drip from his brown face.

"What the hell do you have in that briefcase?" he asked me. Not only was he out of breath, but he also seemed nervous. It seemed that he believed I was carrying explosives in my briefcase.

For some reason, I became very calm, and I said to the officer, "I'm sorry for running, I must have panicked. The only thing in my briefcase is my books and food. I'm on my way to my class at John Jay College."

Now the officer seemed puzzled. He said, "You're a student at John Jay College? I graduated from there."

He was still looking at my briefcase, so I leaned over and opened it for him. Out tumbled my two books on criminal justice and a can of spaghetti and meatballs. The can of spaghetti and meatballs caught his eye. "Why do you have that?" he asked.

"That's my dinner for tonight." In a moment, his face turned into one of absolute sadness. He quickly looked both ways, checking to see if anyone was watching us. We were alone. Then he put his hand in his left pocket, found some change, and handed me two tokens. He said, "Pay your fare next time, okay?"

This officer was putting his own job at risk. I had broken the law and it was his responsibility to either arrest me and take me to the station house or issue me a ticket. Most cops would have. I have no idea why this cop didn't. Instead, he gave me tokens out of his pocket and told me to hurry on to class.

As he put his hand on his gun, he looked down and shook his head. He did not look at me. I heard him say, under his breath, "I almost put a bullet in his back."

I replied very quietly, "I want to thank you for not doing that." Then I turned and went off to my class.

That experience reminded me of the paradox of my struggle. On the one hand, I wanted something meaningful in my life. Yet, my obsession with gambling and the quick path was still a liability. However, my obsession with education inspired me to continue despite the odds. Strangely, I started my undergrad studies at age 19, and when I finished with my four-year degree, I was 35 years old. My obsession was a tug of war. I had to finally give up gambling, to make any real progress with my education. Once I completed my B.S. degree in criminal justice, I decided to apply to law school. Unfortunately, there was not one school that would accept me. It was then I decided to set my sights on other goals, maybe consider earning a Master's degree.

However, as I continued to work with Dr. Wagner I could see I had work to do on myself. I had much to learn about obsessive-compulsive behavior. Then, I had a major breakthrough. I would learn how to combine all of the positive forces in my life. It would be one of the most important lessons about changing negative behavior into positive behavior. It was a lesson about how to re-direct energy towards a positive goal. I would finally learn how to turn the tables on my obsessive-compulsive behavior.

For the first time, I would have a strategy for turning my obsessive-compulsive tendencies into an asset. I decided to return to John Jay College of Criminal Justice to pursuit a Master's degree in public administration. This would be my opportunity to make the transition. This would be my chance to learn if my obsessive-compulsive behavior could be re-directed towards a positive goal.

PUTTING THE ENEMY TO WORK

At the start, I was really doubtful about my chances of being accepted into the Master's program at John Jay College. By 2009, I started to gain some confidence that I could find a way to complete the program. I was fortunate to meet with some of the faculty before the start of my first year. They were extremely encouraging. I was surprised when I was told that my application into the Master's program was approved. I was completely stunned.

I noticed how my self-esteem started to soar. This was the biggest thing to happen to me since my daughter was born. I now understood the power of education. I realized that the chance to earn my Master's degree was "chicken soup for my soul." My self-esteem and sense of self-worth improved greatly. And, I loved being back at John Jay College. Once again I was feeling like a winner, and I did it without gambling.

I was ready to study and work all at the same time. Yet, I was now faced with a challenge. The opportunity to complete a master's degree would involve focus and discipline. I was learning about the power of positive thinking and obsessive-compulsive behavior. I had an opportunity to put some of these principles to a test. I had the chance to use my obsessive-compulsive personality to accomplish a very important goal. I had the opportunity to take something that was a liability, and use it as a tool. I was thinking "it's time to put the enemy to work for me".

I saw this as a part of my transition. I had the time to focus on my new goals. My daughter Maxine had moved away to a college in Rhode Island. She was doing great in school. However, she was living with her then-boyfriend, who she later married. It all happened very quickly. She learned that she was having a baby.

Now, my oldest daughter Juleah had given birth to my granddaughter Tatyanna the year before. I had mixed feeling about becoming a grandfather at age fifty. But, life happens. The world was changing, and I need to find ways to accept the demands in life. I decided to focus on the prospect of furthering my education.

I was told that the Master's program was very challenging. I was advised that it was very difficult to balance studies with a full-time job. However, I now had a secret weapon. It was my illness- my obsessive-compulsive behavior. My obsessive behavior would be a very important tool. However, I also think the sessions with my therapist, Dr. Wagner was really helping me.

The odd thing about going to see a therapist is that you may feel a bit self-conscious, and yet, you feel important. I think I did. I hardly told anyone that I was seeing a private therapist. I would sometimes talk about it with my recovery group. However, I never told any family or any of my friends. Dr. Wagner wanted to help me understand the power of obsession, and the reality of addiction. However, other issues stood in the way of having a better life.

She asked, "Why do you think you have such a difficult time trusting people?". I did not respond for a few seconds. "I am not sure, I just know that I have a big problem with trust, since, I was a teenager, I could not trust people, because, people are unpredictable, people are emotional, and emotions change quickly, and you never know the person you think you know, for example, my ex-wife, I married this woman, and I knew nothing about her, and she had her secrets, we all have our secrets, yet sooner or later the truth will come to light".

Dr. Wagner listened carefully. "What did you learn" I replied, "I learned to not trust people, and to trust my gut, like, during my marriage, I knew that something was wrong, so, I finally search my house, I found some personal letters, my wife was involved with another man, so I read all of her letters, and then I knew that I did not want to be married anymore". Dr. Wagner did not respond. We talked about different issues as well as about trust. However, being able to trust another person will always be a challenge for me.

So, over time I would focus my energy on more tangible goals, like building a business or earning a degree. That was the tradeoff for me. I would not focus my energy on relationships with people, I would focus on achieving a goal. I still had a great deal to learn about how to re-direct that focus and energy. I was running a staffing agency, activating working with nonprofit organizations to help disadvantaged groups, and completing my master's degree.

At times I had some concerns that I was biting off more than I could chew. However, I liked working obsessively, and if I could work seven days a week, I would. I had also gained some confidence in myself and was not struggling so much with anxiety and stress. This time, I was confident that I could completely redirect my energies towards positive goals and balance some of the negative forces in my life.

My plans were not complicated: I would structure my goals, and then commit to those goals and their strategies. I would follow the roadmap that I found reading Napoleon Hill. I would plan my goals, and allow my subconscious mind time to absorb those goals and my commitment —allow myself time to become obsessed with those plans, so to speak. I was using what I learned on those cold nights sleeping in the subways while reading all of the books on positive thinking. It seems that obsession is not just a young man's game. I told myself to believe in the process. I had to apply the principles of persistence and faith.

I would continue to schedule meetings with members of the faculty at John Jay College. In particular, I would meet often with Dr. Stanley Diih. In some ways, he had become my mentor as well as the others. I was fortunate to be a student at John Jay College because the quality of education was outstanding in my view. I talked with students from other schools, and they did not have the type of support I had at John Jay College.

To my surprise, I completed my first year in the Master's program, with a 3.85 GPA. I made the Dean's List. I was speechless. My sense of self-worth was over the moon. I was walking on air. I was beginning to learn about the magic of education. By the second year, my professors had encouraged me to dream even greater dreams. Yet, life was also there to bring me back to reality. I had concerns about money, and business to consider.

In the course of my journey, I also found that success attracts other problems, such as that some people resent seeing you succeed because it makes them feel like they are failing. Rather, some people enjoy seeing you frustrated and defeated. So, I committed to one simple rule: I would avoid, at all costs, getting caught up in other people's games. Instead, I told myself, to avoid playing the game. However, if I must, then I have one rule, "The game is not over until *I* win". Failure was not an option for me anymore.

I completed the Master's program at John Jay College of Criminal Justice in only two years. I received my degree in public administration and achieved a 3.85 GPA. I made the Dean's list both years. It seemed that my theory was correct. I could re-direct my obsessive-compulsive behavior. I could turn a negative into a positive. I could put the enemy to work for me.

Yet, when I received my award from the Dean, it was surprising. I think I was more in shock than my professors. I would continue to have several meetings with my professors. It was as if I developed a new group of advisors. We had discussed every topic you could imagine, including the opportunity for me to teach at a college, or enroll in the doctoral programs. For the first time in my life, I had people acknowledge my ability to be a scholar. It was time to prepare for the next stage in my development.

I added to my obsessive-compulsive behavior the need to be prepared for any opportunity. It fit well with my obsessive tendencies to review my plans constantly. My motto was, "It's better to be prepared for an opportunity and not get one than to get an opportunity you're not prepared for."

Opportunities seldom come in ways that we expect. I learned that I needed to always be alert because an important opportunity might be just around the corner. Sometimes opportunity comes at a moment when you've been completely thrown off and may even feel vulnerable. What I did not realize was that earning my Master's degree was the game changer I waited for all my life. It turns out that it was one of my professors who changed my entire perspective.

To my surprise, I was dating again. I would still see Monique on and off. Yet, I started to enjoy going out on a date. I met a woman named Lisa. We would go out to different restaurants and nightclubs. I was now into going to the theater. I still loved the movie theater, the place was like my sanctuary/ Now, I was going to see shows on Broadway. My favorite shows included "Phantom of the Opera" "Miss Saigon" "The Lion King" and" Chicago". I would take my daughters to see "The King and I" "Beauty and the Beast" and "Les Miserables."

My struggle with the "Big Shot Syndrome" was far from over. But, I was making progress. I was slowly learning to feel good in my own skin. My 12 step recovery group played a big part in my progress. Now, my visits to see Dr. Wagner was combined with my recovery group meeting, which added a real punch to my progress. And, then I made another breakthrough. During one of my weekend retreats, I felt a real connection to my higher power. I always believed in God. But, this was the first time that I felt a real connection. I also realized for the first time that opportunity often comes disguised as disappointment.

I have talked about these concepts many times. But, I had not really embraced this principle. I needed to incorporate this concepts of managing life's challenges. So, I began to really pay attention. Then something occurred. in my final year as a student in the Master's program at John Jay College. Which would be the ultimate example of what I often called "the sly disguise of opportunity"

SLY DISGUISE OF OPPORTUNITY

In 2011, I graduated from the Master's program at John Jay College of Criminal Justice and began looking for any opportunity to teach at a college. I also made another really important decision. I decided to enroll in the doctoral program at a university in New York City. I was once again shocked to learn that I was accepted into the doctoral program at New School University.

The school was located on 14th Street and Sixth Ave in Manhattan. Only a ten-minute ride from my apartment. The school was well known, and I was extremely excited. My sense of self-esteem had improved a great deal, and I even had moments of feeling confident in my chances of success at the school. However, I was still uneasy most of my first year.

I completed my first full year in the doctoral program at the New School on a high note. I had met some great faculty members and my grade point average was 3.85. I was really proud of myself. Yet, at times I could not believe I was actually a doctoral student. They call that "the imposter syndrome".

It was time to face another reality. I was facing some real challenges in business. I even toyed with the idea of re-starting the WBA. I think it was mostly my ego attempting a comeback. It was time to completely abandon any plan to re-open the WBA. My bruised ego and my frustration that the business didn't work had kept me clinging to some hope of a rebound. I had even tried to rework the plans, and find new investors. I tried to convince myself that I could restore the organization and allow the investors to recover their investment. But it was simply too late.

I even met with Dr. Dick Barnett at the famous "Clyde's Wine and Dine" restaurant. I wanted to get his perspective on what was happening in the nonprofit sector and my interest in teaching at a college. We had not talked about the WBA for years.

He sat down, and he took out his laptop. He said, "It's really time to think out of the box." Then he told me, "I'm putting together a proposal to present to Madison Square Garden. My nonprofit organization will develop programs to educate young people about finances and the stock market, because, as you can see, educational programs are really needed."

I did see the need for the type of programs he was putting together, and the way Barnett described his plans sounded like the program could be quite effective. However, I could not remember one time when Madison Square Garden ever supported one of his proposals. So, I commented, "This sounds like a similar plan you put together two years ago to present to Madison Square Garden. They did not make a move then. Why would they make a move now?"

Barnett had pitched this idea of an educational program to the suits at MSG for quite some time, and I did not understand why someone like him, ex-NBA player, two-time NBA World Champion, and member of the Hall of Fame, had not gotten any support. Here's a guy who played fifteen years in the NBA and was a legend before he entered the league. People still knew his name even though he had been retired for over thirty years. Yet, I almost felt like I was talking to Willie Loman in Arthur Miller's *Death of a Salesman.* Why had they not made a move?

I put the question to him, "Barnett, do you ever get the sense that they are just spinning your wheels? You put together at least a dozen plans in the last year, and you're still waiting for their support. Do you really think something will happen this time?"

He considered my questions for a moment. Then, Barnett said, "Everything is motivated by money. People in power will not do anything for you unless it benefits the bottom line. We need to find the right people to support this venture." As he spoke, I noticed something wrong. He did not seem to be the same guy I have known for so many years.

I asked him, "Do you think the response will be different this time around?" Barnett gave me a cautious nod, and said, "This plan is different, maybe even better than the last proposal, because this plan has a broader base in the community."

In some ways, I saw Dick Barnett as the eternal optimist. He didn't see it, but I did. He had a lot of great plans and yet very few came to fruition. Barnett always had great plans. I thought he was throwing darts against a board and hoping something would stick.

As he scrolled on his laptop, Barnett mused, "the politicians today are all about self-interest, the businessmen are looking to fill their pockets, and that's the real deal right now." Then, he seemed to drop his head. That was strange. He fell forward and collapsed onto the table. I jumped up, and called out "We need a doctor?" A lady at the next table said "I am a doctor" She quickly moved his head back, and began to examine Barnett. He was unconscious. I was thinking he may have had a heart attack. Everything seemed to happen quickly. The ambulance and medics arrived in a few minutes. They moved him into the ambulance, and I followed in a taxi. By the time we reached Roosevelt Hospital, he was alert again. It was a close call.

I waited around to hear from the doctor. I was able to provide some information about which family member to contact. I then took a seat in the waiting room. I glanced up at the television. On the news was another story about a large company going out of business.

It was a challenging time for most people and everyone was looking at the man in the White House for answers. That happened to be President Barack Obama. The stock markets and financial markets were still unstable but the spirits of millions of black men like myself were still riding high. President Obama was sending a message to every black man, both young and old, about why it is important to dream. Hopefully, it's a dream that the next person can believe in with you.

It was as if we could hear an echo of Dr. Martin Luther King Jr. making that incredible speech on August 28, 1963. If we didn't understand then what Dr. Martin Luther King had envisioned for the future, then we learned that lesson on the day when Barack Obama raised his right hand to take the oath of office.

Like every other black man in America, my eyes were glued to the television on January 20th, 2009. It was the single most historic moment of my life. It would not have mattered much if I were still unemployed or running my own company or homeless.

It was a day to be proud to be a black man, and so it was not a coincidence that I continued to press on to reinvent myself. Opportunity is everywhere.

The doctor walked into the waiting room. He told me that Barnett would need to remain in the hospital for a few days. However, he was feeling better. I was just glad I was with him when he collapsed. I thanked the doctor for the update. While I was waiting, I had a conversation with a man who managed a nonprofit organization in Harlem. He was at the hospital visiting a sick relative. We exchanged business cards. His name was Carlo. I told him that we should schedule a meeting the next week. Then, I walked outside to take a cab home.

Carlo also happened to be the director of a workforce development program that provided job training for young, black men in Harlem. That was important to me because for my doctoral studies I had decided to research the unemployment experiences of young black men. Carlo would become my entrance into that issue. His connection to the workforce development program let me design a case study there. I would not have had the opportunity to meet Carlo if not for the misfortune of Dick Barnett being rushed to the hospital

Because of Carlo's help, I would later be able to complete my doctoral studies. So once again, the lesson of the "sly disguise of opportunity" was quite apparent.

Or maybe, it was the fact that I was learning how to change a negative situation into an asset. I was finally learning how to turn liabilities, into a resource. I was starting to learn the magic of education, and how earning a degree was "chicken soup for the soul".

It seemed that all of the work to restore my self-esteem was finally taking hold. For the first time in my life, I would greet people with a smile, and a warm handshake. In the past, there was very little eye contact, and I was always feeling on edge or stressed. My hands were always cold. I was oftentimes uneasy. Now, I felt different. I smiled more. Something had changed. I knew that my weekly 12 step meeting was helping. I knew that my visits to Dr. Wagner were also a benefit to my recovery. Yet, something else was happening to me. To my surprise the answers was right in front of me the whole time.

PART THREE

CHAPTER 7

"We stand today on the edge of a New Frontier ... the frontier of unknown opportunities and perils, the frontier of unfilled hopes and unfilled threats."

President John F. Kennedy

A HISTORIC BREAKTHROUGH

My first year as a doctoral student at the New School University was quite overwhelming. Yet, I somehow maintained a 3.85 GPA. To add to my astonishment, I was contacted to teach my first class as a college professor. When I walked into the Borough of Manhattan Community College to teach my first class, my spirit soared like an eagle. I was nervous, of course, but I had never in my life felt so good about myself. I found that teaching nurtured my sense of self-worth and self-esteem. I was truly proud of myself. I trusted that if BMCC had selected me to teach this class, it was an indication of my value as a person.

For the first time, I was making the connection. For me, this was a monumental breakthrough. I finally realized that the combination of my 12 step recovery meeting, my weekly appointments with my therapist, and my twice-a-year weekend retreats provided a foundation for a new way of thinking and living. I even found less of a need for the nightlife. I was growing bored with the nightclub scene. Now, I was meeting people in network meetings and business conferences. I even when out on a few dates.

However, the real sign of progress I could feel in my soul. When I walked into the classroom, the students looked at me curiously. I'm not sure if this was because of my suit and tie, or because I was African-American. A black male professor was not often seen at this school.

Or, perhaps, they simply could sense my uncertainty. However, something gave me another boost to my spirit that day. When one of the students said, “Good evening, Professor Williams,” I felt the ever-familiar adrenaline rush. I was still a bit nervous. I was feeling uneasy.

By the time I arrived home that night, I was a bit out of sorts. I was struggling with this sense of inadequacy. Some of my old demons decided to visit me. In particular, Mr. Low Self- Esteem wanted to talk to me. He started to get into my ear. Then, I had an overwhelming feeling that I would be discovered to be a fraud. Some call this the “imposter syndrome.” The signs of the condition include chronic self-doubt, anxiety, and negative self-talk.

What strikes me about this condition is that most people struggle with these feelings despite overwhelming evidence of their capabilities.

Maybe I should not have been surprised when I found myself struggling in the same way. However, this time I was not so quick to give in. I also felt that my students were getting a lot out of the class.

I had wanted to teach at a college for some time, and after completing my Master's degree, I believed I was ready. So, I reached out to a contact at a local community college. That is how I became an adjunct professor at BMCC.

Now, my goal was to complete my doctoral studies and then seek a full-time faculty position at John Jay College. This next chapter of my life involved a new stage of human development, which included the world of education and learning. President John F. Kennedy once spoke about the new frontier. For me, education was that frontier. I knew I would always be a student of life and an educator for as long as possible.

I had believed that great things would happen once I got in the classroom. In my mind, it would be another chapter in my life and another sign of the changing times. I saw that the world was evolving and I needed to keep in step. Even now, I still feel the excitement of having witnessed the election of the first black president in the history of the United States. President Obama was a powerful role model for me. I was determined to believe that I could be a good professor.

So, I was beginning to tackle the imposter syndrome in my own way. I reached out to one of my professors from John Jay College. Dr. Rubie Malone was my very first professor when I was a freshman at John Jay College.

We talked on the phone a week before the semester started. I said, "Dr. Malone, I have the opportunity to teach a class at BMCC, but I'm struggling a bit with my confidence and feeling ill-prepared for the task. I thought I'd reach out to you because I remember our first class together and how important it was for me."

Dr. Malone listened carefully and then responded, "Michael, I hope you realize that what you have to offer your students is unique. You are bringing not only your knowledge to the table but your life experiences. I understand the struggle with confidence. We all experience that on some level."

She continued, "We know about self-doubt, but remember that it is your personal experience that is so valuable. Since I suspect many of your students will be people of color, I think you will do quite well in your first semester."

I thanked her for her encouragement. "I have a feeling that as the semester progresses, I'll be calling you again for your guidance."

"Michael," she said in response, "I think it is great we made this connection. As we've been speaking, I had a flashback to my first time arriving here in New York City. I felt so out of place, but I decided to keep my faith and believe in myself, and I knew that things would work out. Then, when I walked into John Jay, I knew that I was in the right place."

I had to agree with her. There is something inspirational about John Jay College of Criminal Justice. I told her I thought it was the people. I thanked her again for taking the time to talk to me. Becoming a college professor was a big deal for me, and such a new experience, but our conversation had revved me up to start the first semester.

Dr. Malone laughed and said, "Yes, well, you'll get used to being called Professor Williams. And soon I'll be calling you Dr. Williams, I have that much confidence in you. Just remember to keep the faith. It's not a question of *if* you will finish your dissertation, but of *when* you will finish your dissertation." Her words would carry me for the next decade.

I would sometimes struggle with the imposter syndrome through my time as a professor. However, my confidence was beginning to take hold. I was doing the basics, and that was important. I was always thinking about ways for building self-esteem and making character changes. However, this time I had a new definition of what "self-inventory" and "self-worth" meant.

The early years of building my self-esteem were about feeling better about myself and projecting a different image to people. It was time to go further and develop a framework for real self-improvement. I believed when Napoleon Hill said that "thoughts are things," so I realized I needed to develop a deeper consciousness of the things that dominated my thoughts.

I also remembered the words, "When one is ready for a thing, it puts in its appearance"

I needed to do more than be hopeful and think positive. I needed to see myself as a college professor, successful, and well respected. I needed to organize myself like a college professor. I needed to talk, walk, and smell like a college professor.

I also paid close attention to my interactions with other people. I had to remember lessons about stereotypes. Some still had doubts about my chances as a college professor. I would think about the pros and cons. So, I put everything down on paper because committing my thoughts to paper gives them a more tangible form. Once again, I made daily lists of my A-to-Z goals for personal growth. I especially wanted to have a plan for developing a relationship with a mentor.

I was finally able to call Dick Barnett after he returned home from the hospital. Over the years, I had many good conversations with Dr. Barnett about personal development and about how he managed that process. I once asked him, "Are you surprised that people still have difficulty believing that you went from a professional athlete to a scholar?"

He replied, "I'm not so concerned with what they think. My focus must be on my goals. I keep the future in front of me."

That's the problem with many people, people spend most of their time looking behind them. They live in the past. The key to success is to look ahead, no matter what happens.

When he wrote his first book of poems, I told him I was inspired by his poetry. Dr. Barnett smiled and said, "Life is all about transformation. Everything in life is a transition. I'm just having some fun with it."

I hung on every word. Dr. Barnett made sense to me. His perspective about looking forward was the best piece of advice that I had heard in a long time. He also taught me to aim high; it is better to shoot for the moon because if you don't get that far you will still land among the stars. I took Dr. Barnett's advice.

Soon, I was actually looking forward to teaching my class at BMCC. I took pride in my work. I let my obsessive-compulsive behavior take over, and drive me to prepare for each lesson. Now, I was obsessed with the idea of being the best college professor that I could be. The real question was could that make a difference as I continued my journey to complete my Ph.D.

UNIVERSITY OF HARD KNOTTS

The first year in the doctoral program at the New School was great, and then the problems started. I had my first experience with a member of the faculty who was clearly a racist. He told me indirectly that I did not belong in the Ph.D. program at the school. I was in shock. I thought about how to best approach this situation. I did not want to jump to any conclusions. Yet, I did not realize that he was determined that I not complete my degree.

In 2011, the world was changing before my eyes. President Barack Obama announced that the founder and leader of Al-Qaeda, Osama bin Laden had been killed. It was also an election year, and Mitt Romney would be the Republican Party candidate. Then, I read in the paper, that Steve Jobs has died, at the age of 56. I tell myself that Steve Jobs was a man who knew a great deal about obsession. He learned to re-direct that obsession, and yet, it seems he may have paid a high price. My obsession was to do quite well in the doctoral program. But, now I faced a challenge.

When I first considered entering the doctoral program, I took the time to talk to people in the know, including my professors. I asked a few of them to meet with me over a cup of coffee. I was still considering what school or program would be best for me to pursue a doctoral degree. I decided to continue with the process based on advice and encouragement I received from some faculty members at John Jay College, most notably Dr. Stanley Diih and Dr. Peters.

Dr. Stanley Diih was one of my former professors at John Jay College. He had come to the United States from Senegal. We met in one of my very first classes in the master's program.

Dr. Diih shared his view about the importance of doctoral studies with every student. It seemed that Dr. Diih wanted every student to enroll in the Ph.D. program at John Jay College. I'm not sure how many students were interested, but I do know that I was extremely impressed by what he told me.

After the first class, I approached Dr. Diih to talk to him about his lecture. I actually told him about my early years in the South Bronx and living on the streets. He shared with me some of his life experiences in Senegal. We seemed to make a connection.

I said, "Dr. Diih, I'm considering your suggestions regarding the doctoral program. However, I've had a difficult time over the years and still struggle at times with self-doubt. To be honest with you, I initially enrolled at John Jay College in 1978, and I did not graduate until 1993. It took me fifteen years to complete my undergraduate degree. During that time I lost jobs and even ended up homeless. However, I continued to attend school with the hope that I would one day graduate. So I am interested in what you shared with the class"

Dr. Diih listened to me carefully and did not even appear surprised when I revealed that I had once been a homeless man. He didn't even blink. Dr. Diih stood about 5'7" and had a good build. He looked like he regularly worked out in the gym. During his discussions in the class, he had informed us that he was a Detective Sergeant with the NYPD. Yet, he wore glasses and in some way reminded me of Martin Luther King, Jr. His voice was soft and he never raised his voice, even when he was excited about a topic.

After I had described my feelings about entering the doctoral program, he said in a reassuring voice, "Mr. Williams, what you have told me already answers any question regarding your abilities to succeed in the doctoral program. You just revealed to me that you persisted despite all odds and opposition. You chose to return to John Jay College even when you were homeless, and even after you were married and raising a family. You've chosen to pursue your dream, and because of your faith and determination, you can achieve your goal. That is exactly what you need to succeed in the doctoral program, and I say to you right now, I have absolutely no doubt that you can make it."

He also promised me, "I'll do anything I can to help you."

Listening to Dr. Diih, I felt the excitement and the adrenaline rush once again. For the first time, I had found someone who believed that I could earn a Ph.D. Dr. Diih was making me think that I could achieve a dream that had seemed almost impossible.

Years later, as I was starting my dissertation process, I met Dr. Diih again and he reinforced his sense of confidence in me. I was developing a framework for my research and one of the key components of that framework were the people around me.

For example, I had to remind myself that it was never too late to pursue my dreams. In 2008, when I met Dr. Diih, I was already fifty years old and was not sure I could consider the four years it would take to complete my Ph.D. I was told on several occasions that I was getting too old for school and that I should put these plans aside. People like Dr. Diih reassured me that was not the case.

He said, "Mr. Williams, I understand your concerns about how much time is involved. However, Mr. Williams, if by the grace of God you're going to be fifty-five anyway, why not have a Ph.D.?"

I also met with another professor at John Jay College, who was a bit more candid. My last meeting with Dr. Peters still stands out in my mind. I enjoyed her classes back in the day and learned a few things from her style of teaching. I decided to meet with her before enrollment into the doctoral program.

I was sitting in her office and I said, "Professor Peters, I've given it a lot of thought and I really think I should pursue my doctoral degree. I feel very strongly that I can use my work experience in the field of employment services and my many years working with young black men to develop a case study. I think that young black men face a unique set of challenges as they enter the job market and I think a study would have some value. Based on my experience in the master's program, I feel that I'm ready to take on this challenge. But, I'm looking for all the advice I can get from the people who would know."

Dr. Peters listened to me very intently. When she began to speak, she seemed to choose her words very carefully. She told me, "Yes, I do see the potential in you. I've seen it from the very first time you were in my class and when we've had the opportunity to talk. You've told me about your life and work experiences. So, I can certainly see how that would be very relevant."

"Yes, as I sit here looking at you right now, I can actually see it, I can see you as a doctoral candidate," she continued. I was now feeling quite good about my decision. Then she said, "I do have one question for you. Why on earth would you want to do this to yourself?"

Huh?

I did my best not to appear puzzled, and I did not have the presence of mind to ask Dr. Peters what she meant by that. However, eight-and-a-half years later, after I've completed my dissertation, I think I know exactly what she meant.

The lessons I would learn in my doctoral program would start early on and would be quite insidious. These lessons would inform precisely with what Dr. Peters was referring to. I now understand that she was asking me why I wanted to experience what was likely going to be the most difficult thing I could take on. In other words, nobody ever says that the doctoral journey is pleasant.

My first four years as a doctoral student provided some keen insights for me as well as some perspective regarding Dr. Peters' question. I guess the doctoral journey became my next obsession. However, by the fourth year, I had some deep regrets. It was more than merely not pleasant—it was cruel.

I started my doctoral studies at the New School University. It was exciting to become a student at that school. I was told that the New School was a great institution, and I did quite a bit of research before starting the application and admissions process. As anyone would imagine, I was surprised to be accepted into their doctoral program. In my first year, I met some really great faculty members who were not only supportive but seemed to encourage students of color to pursue their dreams. I was very enthusiastic after that first year.

Unfortunately, I was soon confronted once by racism in a way that I never expected. I was told by one of the most senior faculty members in the doctoral program that I did not fit the model of a Ph.D. candidate or a New School graduate. It was implied that it was my choice to take all the classes I wanted at the New School. I was welcome to spend all the money that I wanted for tuition. However, I was told that when it was time for graduation, I should not expect to be in the graduating class. The first time I hear this I was shunned. I had experienced racism before, somehow, this was different. I was now confronting racism head-on.

I was not, in that person's opinion, the model of a Ph.D. candidate. What made this all the more depressing was the fact that while some faculty members wanted to support my efforts in the doctoral program, the faculty members who had the authority demonstrated to me that I wasting my time. To be confronted by this reality at the end of my four years was difficult. And just as I was preparing to start my dissertation, too—that was completely devastating

I was depressed and frustrated by that experience, yet I told no one about it. I felt that people were tired of hearing about racism. I was also concerned about being accused of playing the race card. Oddly, it was 2016, the year we elected Donald Trump. However, the people who really know me, and who know about my life experiences, would know that I am not one to play the race card. I just wanted to complete my degree.

However, soon, I did meet with a group of attorneys to discuss a lawsuit. They were willing to take the case, but I was advised that the process would be long and expensive. It was a difficult decision.

I needed to do some real soul-searching. I had to choose between starting a lawsuit against the school, which would occupy the next three or four years, or consider transferring to another school to complete my dissertation.

After a period of deep reflection, I decided to transfer out of the New School and complete my dissertation elsewhere. However, during the process of selecting another university, I learned that I would need to repeat most of the coursework I had already done. The process that should've taken me four years to complete would instead take more than eight.

I was angry but I felt that I had no choice, so I agreed. Yet, I was very bitter. Not only was it frustrating to be confronted by racism in an institution like the New School, I felt a great deal of anger about the fact that it was one of the most expensive universities in the country and I was not allowed to transfer all of my credits. I felt that one day the truth should be told.

However, I still believed that I could earn a Ph.D. one day. This was not my first setback in life. I had experienced many challenges from my days as a homeless man, struggles with gambling addiction, and even my years as a business entrepreneur. In a way, all of these experiences prepared me for this day. So, once again I used the principles and strategies of persistence, faith, and determination that I needed to press on.

The year before I decided to talk with the one person who always gave me the best advice. My mother Mary Alice James. She was so much that I decided to continue my education. However, her health was failing. We had a few really bad years. Then, we lost my brother Ronnie. Those years were very difficult. But, my mom Mary was always there for me. In a way, I always had the love of a mother. She told me not to give up on my studies. I told her that I would continue to pursue my degree. Unfortunately, her health continued to deteriorate. In 2015, the day before Christmas she passed away. For the second time in my life, I would attend a funeral for my mother.

I resolved that I would not allow the experiences at the New School to stop me from pursuing my dream. I also decided not to pursue the lawsuit against the New School. I would simply transfer to another school and continue my doctoral studies. My mother once told me "You must pick your battles carefully".

Later that year, it was my good fortune to be accepted into the Ph.D. program in public policy and public administration at Walden University. Gladly, I found it to be a much better program than at the other school. As a result, I became a more proficient and prolific researcher.

SCHOLARS ON THE STREET

I transferred to Walden University in the fall of 2016. Despite the setbacks at the New School, I was excited to continue my doctoral journey. I had mixed emotions. I was feeling some anger. I had spent four years at that school. Then, I was told that I was being dropped from the program. So, finding another school was a big deal. Now, I was feeling great about my prospects. I was using all the tools that I had gained from all of the years before. I was using everything I learned from Napoleon Hill, I was using my lessons in persistence. I combined my desire, with my faith. I was now teaching at a college, operating a staffing agency, and studying for my Ph.D. Not bad for a guy who once was sleeping in the subways.

However, the Melville staffing agency that I worked for was becoming increasingly unstable and I was aware of the fact that my continued employment was in question. This caused tremendous frustration for me. It had been part of the reason why I had resisted selling the company in the first place. Little did I know that this was just the start of some of the challenges I would face.

When I had completed the merger with the Melville firm, I understood that I had limited options. The financial crisis had changed the entire sector for the staffing industry. I hoped that I had selected the right group to merge my company with. I hoped that they had integrity and that they would treat me fairly. I was correct at first. However, after some years had passed, it was clear that things had changed. Some of the partners who were there at the start of the merger were now gone. There was new management, and a different perspective driving the agency.

I felt it was time to think "out of the box" Maybe it was time to open a new company. I had several factors working in my favor if I decided to open my company again. I had a strong network group of people who could help a person starting a new business. I could also consider working full-time at a university. I decided to turn to my network group first.

Some years before I had joined the Professional Network Group (PNG), a group of men and women professionals from different sectors of the business world. The group consisted of about twenty-four people, both business owners, and executives. We had one of everything in the group. In our network was one person who operated an accounting firm, another person who was a banker, another who an attorney, and one or two who may have owned their own tech companies. I was the individual who represented employment and staffing services.

That was my main network group. I had also developed what I call my "Core Network Group", which was simply a group of professional people from different industries who shared information and referrals amongst themselves. However, my group had an additional layer. The individuals in this group were people with who I not only shared business information and referrals but who were also members of my support recovery group.

This allowed me to work with professionals who knew about my journey from a homeless man to a businessman. They knew me as a person in recovery as well as a business contact. Because these were individuals who had a personal relationship with me and each other, we felt a vested interest in each other's success.

I often turned to Dave S. when I needed motivation and inspiration. I always felt better after having a conversation with Dave, and he was my go-to person when I had to make important decisions. When I started itching to re-open my United Personnel Agency, I called him and told him that I would like to come by his office for a cup of coffee. He said he would be free in the afternoon.

Dave had really come a long way in life. His office took up almost the entire floor in a building on 23rd and Sixth Avenue. When I arrived at his office, I looked out the large windows onto Sixth Ave and saw a swarm of busy people moving about. I felt a little guilty about troubling Dave because I knew he was probably very busy. Dave had hit rock bottom thirty years before and then found recovery. Despite all of his success, he remains a humble and down-to-earth guy.

So I said to him, “I'm having some real problems at work. There have been management changes, different people are making decisions, and I don't have a good feeling about how things are going. I feel like my position is compromised. What do you think about that?”

Dave thought for a moment. Then he replied, very honestly, “Mike, things are always changing. That's the nature of the business: nothing stays the same. That's why guys like me and you need to live one day at a time. I understand you're concerned, especially with the changes going on at your agency, but if you decide to go back on your own and start your own company again, you’ll be going back to a whole different dynamic. It’s been years since you’ve had to put out fires every day. Do you remember how to do it? Are you sure you’re ready for that again, Mike?”

What Dave said was true. It had been many years since I had run my own business. The last year of doing so was the most stressful time in my life. And now, we were living in a different world. If I did restart my company, I needed to think about financing and building up my clients again.

I waited a moment before responding. “Dave, I’ve been thinking about that a lot, especially about the time and energy that would be required to get the company going. I’m also not sure about the financing. Some of my clients are sending me mixed signals about whether we will continue to do business in the future. And, I should mention, I am currently studying for a doctoral degree.”

Dave replied “I knew you were teaching at the college, but you mean you returned to school again? That’s fantastic! I just want you to think about how you are planning things right now. It sounds like you may be putting too much on your plate. Put your ego aside for the time being and think pragmatically. If you have to leave the company or if they terminate your employment, you could easily go to work for another company.”

Dave was making a lot of sense. He continued, “What company would not want to hire you right now? You have twenty-five years of experience in the staffing business, and during that time you only worked for two companies. That is a hell of a track record and I think anybody would give you a job. Be realistic.”

Dave had been glancing at his watch and I knew it is lunchtime. I decided not to push my luck. However, Dave suggested, "Let's go to the Outback Steakhouse." We talked a bit more over lunch. I decided to take his advice. I would not make any big moves. Just hang on for now.

These were the types of lessons I learned from the people in my universal network, the perspectives, and insights they provided me. I see them as scholars on the streets, and they often taught me things I could not have learned at a university. The most important street scholar for me was my good friend Phil Baumgarten.

I've already mentioned Phil, my accountant. We had been together from the beginning and I would've told anybody we were the best of friends. However, Phil did not tell me he was dying of cancer in 2017. He even filed my tax return for me the way he always did, and then his wife Esther called to tell me that he had died on April 15. I had not even known he was sick.

Phil was the one person who changed my destiny. If he had not organized the first group of investors, I would never have been CEO of United Personnel Agency. We were close friends and survived many battles in the business world. So, it came as a shock to me to learn that he was dying. Even while we talked on the phone, he never said a word. I still consider him one of my best friends, and I miss him a great deal.

Another longtime friend that I knew from junior high school, Fred Thornton. He is still a valuable contact and network partner. Fred worked with some of the top law firms in New York and always directed business to my company. We also had a lot of fun just going out to bars and clubs. He even joined my family for a cruise once. When you've known someone for almost fifty years, it's hard not to feel part of the family.

My friend Andy up in Mount Kisco, New York, was one of the first people to allow me to develop as a sales executive in the employment business. Andy was a great network partner, confidant, and friend. I enjoyed our years of working together because we never had a problem with ego. Andy eventually worked out of my office when I became President of United Personnel Agency.

I also was fortunate to meet a lady at one of the large unions in New York City. Sandra was the manager of District 1199's union, and she became one of my key contacts in business as well as someone I could confide in. Over the years we became good friends. It is rare to meet someone who works with you during both good and bad times. If not for Sandra, United Personnel Agency would have gone out of business long before the merger. Even after the merger, Sandra continued to work for me. Without her contact, I'm certain I could not have maintained levels of productivity at that agency. Sandra was the most integral part of my network, and one of the main reasons why I was able to remain in business.

I met Sobeyda, a sales representative that I worked for Cable & Wireless, She was another important network partner. She always supported my business efforts and helped keep my spirits up when the road got bumpy. She was a great salesperson, a source of inspiration, and a motivational force.

My coworker and lifelong friend Jeff was a great resource for implementing strategies. The sales environment can be very competitive, even among coworkers, and I benefitted from having someone I could turn to for support and encouragement.

Jeff was exactly that person and never gave in to the cutthroat mentality that exists in the world of sales. I was fortunate to meet someone like Jeff.

Leith was another great contact who had an extensive background in project management. When I met Leith, I did not realize that she would become a great resource for networking as well as one of my clients. She was one of only a few women that I knew who operated their own project management company. Because I respected her, I invited her as a guest speaker for one of my classes at John Jay College.

Another very important contact in my life was Beverly. She was a manager at a major law firm. I met her in the fall of 1998 and she became a key resource for me in business as well as a confidant and a close friend. She was another person who has stood with me in both good and bad times. She consistently directed business to me and enabled me to build my company. I am certain that without her help my business would not have survived the 2008 financial crisis.

I was able to develop a strong network with good friends like Kevin Jones, Jay Reddy, Willie Wimber, Matt Mayo, Jason Wallace, Ruben Sutton, Lucien Mesilas, and Jeanine. People who changed the direction of my life. I also developed strong relationships with nonprofit organizations and community groups.

The value of developing these network groups could not be measured over these many years. I realize that if not for these individuals and groups, I would have not been able to continue in business or experience any real success. It would've been impossible to pursue any of my other goals or dreams. I learned that by developing a strong network group, I was able to change my destiny. Of all the important lessons learned, the lessons about the importance of networking were the most valuable.

I have met some of the best people during those years. I've been encouraged by these people. Their knowledge and experience taught me how to live life better. I had re-connected with Monique who was now living near Atlantic City. It would feel a bit strange taking a bus to visit her. But, for some reason, we managed to stay in touch over the years. I still needed time to focus on other issues. So, we made it work.

I was off to a good start at Walden University. I was having problems at work, but I was still making a living. I was able to visit Maxine and Juleah and enjoy some time with my grandkids. I still had a lot of unfinished business. I had good people around me and they gave good advice. However, the key to the process of self-improvement is learning, and the key to learning is repetition. Repetition is the key to everything. So, what they taught me, I repeated. This is worth repeating: the mother of learning is repetition.

CHAPTER 8

"if I have the belief that I can do it, I shall surely acquire the capacity to do it, even if I may not have it at the beginning"

Mahatma Gandhi

MOTHER OF LEARNING

The year 2016 was truly a mixed bag. The United States seemed to do a one-hundred-and-eighty-degree turn. To this day, I still struggle to comprehend everything that happened then. On the one hand, I was thankful to have found a great institution. I was proud to be accepted into the doctoral program at Walden University and believed that I had found a great school at which to complete my doctoral studies.

I had also decided to write my first book. The book would be called "From The A Train to Ph.D." Once I completed the first draft, I send it to a few family members to read. I then send the draft to a few friends. The pushback was shocking. I was told not to write the book. I think some expected that I would be ashamed of my past. I was not. I was determined to write the book. I believed that my story could help others who were struggling. I still believe that "those who forget the past are doomed to repeat it" and "You are only as sick as the secrets you keep."

That year I was also thrilled to learn that my daughter Maxine had connected with Hillary Clinton and had joined her campaign for President of the United States. Maxine was watching a program about Hillary, and became upset. The program did not paint a good picture of the things that Clinton felt were important for the country. Maxine felt after watching such a negative message about Hillary, that she would write Hillary a letter. Maxine was not naïve.

She knew that Hillary would likely never see her letter and that Clinton received tons of letters every day. Maxine was wrong, the letter was read by Hillary, and Clinton wrote Maxine back. They made a connection. Maxine was even selected to be a delegate for Clinton's campaign in Philadelphia. When they announced my daughter's name on the monitor, I was so proud to be her father. I felt like the luckiest man in the world.

Then—! The nightmare started. I knew that Maxine was convinced that Hillary would win. On the night of the election, my eyes were glued to the TV. Maxine was at the Javits Center. I am not sure if she spoke to Hillary. Then the news came that they had lost. Donald Trump would be the next President of the United States.

After the election, my daughter seemed to descend into a state of sadness. I also was completely dumbfounded by the results of the election and didn't know how to console her. I am not often someone who is at a loss for words, but this time I was speechless. She began to look for job opportunities outside the U.S. She eventually took her children and moved to Bermuda.

Then the problems started at work again. Another change in management led to another wave of downsizing. They also implemented a round of salary cuts. I was understandably angry about this and met with a lawyer and accountant to explore my options for starting a new company.

However, before I put my plan into action, I consulted my recovery support group. There is a saying in the recovery rooms, "Be aware of disappointments and frustrations because they can create an urge to gamble." Under the kind of pressure that I was experiencing, I wanted to discuss what we call" triggers". No matter how often I may try to forget it, I will always be a compulsive gambler.

They told me to be careful. So once again, I went back to basics. I did not make any quick moves. However, it was clear to me that it was time to evaluate the situation and maybe start my own company again. If I did decide to re-open, then I should follow the "roadmap" that I developed years ago.

I remembered an author and motivational speaker named Tom Hopkins. He once said that "Repetition is the mother of learning." I've read Hopkins' book "How to Master the Art of Selling" over a dozen times. He said the only way we truly learn anything is by repeating a process over and over again because the mind does not always make a distinction between what you feed it.

The mind will take whatever it gets, and whatever goes in then comes out. But it starts with repetition. So, it is important to be careful about what goes into your mind. Remember "Junk in, means Junk out".

This was another breakthrough for me. This was a strategy for learning. I could change negative circumstances into positive ones. However, I needed to remember the name of the mother of learning, and her name was "Ms. Repetition".

Whatever my plans, I just need to repeat and repeat and repeat. The plans will become reality, no matter how big or small.

I take this to mean that the subconscious mind may not distinguish between what is good or bad, or difficult or easy. To the subconscious mind, there is no difference between a person becoming homeless or becoming the President of the United States. Rather, if a person dreams small, their subconscious mind achieves small. If they dream big, their subconscious moves to achieve big things.

I had lived the life of both a homeless man and of a chief executive officer and corporate president for several years. And, I can tell you, living the life of a homeless man required a great deal more effort. I'm sure to the rational mind this does not make sense, and yet the only way to truly know would be to have experienced both realities. I have done that. My homeless years were more exhausting and produced diminishing returns in the end. Being a loser was hard work.

On the other hand, my years as a corporate executive and president of the staffing agency were also exhausting, stressful, and all-consuming; yet, the result was that I soon lived in a world that resembled my dreams. Human beings are built to do big things, sometimes great things. So if we do nothing, we're actually going against the grain and lying to ourselves.

John F. Kennedy could have had a fun life, and never entered politics. Someone once asked him, before he became president, "Mr. Kennedy, Why would you go into politics? You are a young, handsome man, and you are very wealthy. Why not just enjoy your money and have a good time in life?"

John F. Kennedy replied, "A life of leisure is the most difficult job in the world." I've thought about those words and what they meant for many years. Kennedy was saying that doing nothing with your life is hard work.

So, I read Tom Hopkins's book many times. My OCD had kicked in. I was fascinated by what Hopkins' book revealed to me in terms of the power of learning. It agreed with the teachings of my mentors. For example, it hearkens back to what I learned from Dr. Barnett about the Five C's. The first C involves *conceiving* a vision for your goals.

The others require writing that vision down and reading it every day. So, I returned to my habit of drafting out my plans and taping them somewhere I would see them every day. Again, I would repeat and repeat and repeat.

My life contains example after example that supports Hopkins' approach. At the beginning of my life as a businessman, I had great difficulty envisioning myself as a corporate executive and the owner of a staffing agency. However, I wrote down my plans and followed my roadmap, and eventually, my plans and my goals reached my subconscious mind. I would often wake up from my sleep and realize that I had been dreaming about my new company. I would immediately write down everything, new ideas or plans, on paper so that I would not forget them.

I would then review my notes every day to keep my plans fresh in my consciousness. It took nine years, but what started as just an idea in my mind became a reality. When I started my first firm, United Personnel Agency, Inc., in March 1991. I received a statement from Phil which confirmed that the company was generating millions of dollars a year. Every plan started with a vision, and then the process of repetition.

My next example, the creation of the Worldwide Basketball Association, provides an even stronger case. I was simply sharing a cup of coffee in my office with Dick Barnett and Phil Baumgarten, and we began talking about the idea of a corporate sports league and nonprofit organization that provided services to the community. I wrote down everything that was said about the design and implementation of such a program. I repeated my plans to myself each day, and at night, I dreamed about my plans. Based on that one meeting, we created the corporation Worldwide Basketball Association, and we were soon were providing services to the community.

My final example is much more complex and painful. I envisioned myself as a college professor and completing a Ph.D. Then, I had spent four-and-a-half years of my life in the doctoral program at the New School. My first three years at the school had been enlightening and I met some wonderful faculty members. However, after I was confronted with racism, I had to decide between pursuing a lawsuit or continuing my doctoral journey. I did not see a way to do both. However, my vision had reached my subconscious mind. So, I had to make it a reality.

I could have left the New School a bitter man and given up on my goals. I could have followed the lawsuit for a few years, and hope to recover a settlement. Instead, I remembered the words of Frank Sinatra, he said "the best revenge in life is massive success." Because my dreams had reached into my subconscious mind, I decided to continue my doctoral studies at another university.

I wanted a program that would allow me to earn my Ph.D. in both public policy and public administration. As I reviewed different schools, I became concerned that the quality of the educational programs at some schools was not on the same level as the New School. To my surprise, I then found Walden University. The quality of the programs and education at Walden seemed better than I had expected. I also met outstanding members of the faculty who seemed to encourage students to pursue their dreams.

I was trusting my instincts again and decided to follow the road that would lead me towards my educational vision. It seemed that as I continued to pursue my educational goals, my self-esteem was improving. Once again, I was learning that education was "chicken soup for the soul". Now, I also found the magic. So, I pursued my degree even harder. I saw another vision. And, I believed that something magical waited at the end of that road.

THE MAGIC OF EDUCATION

By 2017, I felt more and more optimistic about enrolling at Walden University. But why? Was it the university or teaching at a college, or something else that was shining a light in my life? I think I knew the answer. Again, I was finding education to be magical. Every time I walked into the classroom to teach, my self-esteem soared like an eagle. I had found a magic formula for healing the human spirit. It was right in front of me all the whole time. The power of learning, and for some, the power of teaching contains the magic.

However, the start of the year was challenging. My daughter Maxine seemed to fall into a state of depression after the election. Then, in January, Trump's inauguration was on television. I did not see the whole thing, even though the entire speech was 16 minutes. It seemed like the FBI started their investigation before the speech was over. I was simply concerned about my little girl. Maxine had two beautiful kids. Arianna and Jayden were the light in my life. Yet, I knew that Maxine was not a happy camper anymore. I did my best to make things better for her.

Then, I decided to cheer myself up by going to my favorite place, the movie. I decided to see “Molly's Game” with Jessica Chastain and “Darkest Hour” with Gary Oldman. I know, sounds odd. By now, I fancy myself as some type of historian. Oldman won the Oscar for this portray of Winston Churchill.

It seemed that the mood of the country had shifted too. I found myself not watching the news as much. I even avoided discussions in my classes that involved politics. It was a strange time, and yet, I was feeling excited about my progress at Walden University. I had attended a residency, and the experience of meeting faculty was empowering to me. Now, I felt that I could achieve my dreams.

However, I still had my struggles with self-worth and self-esteem. It seems that you must continue to work on these areas in your life, and there is no graduation day. For some reason, I still had trouble accepting the good things taking place in my life. My old demons would talk to me from time to time. In particular, the ghost of self-doubt would rear his ugly head at times. However, something truly magical happened to me.

I was offered an opportunity to teach at the John Jay College of Criminal Justice. This was amazing. I had completed both my undergraduate degree and my master's degree at John Jay College. I could not believe that I could be a candidate for the adjunct professor position. I knew that if I could become a professor at John Jay College that would be a game-changer.

Yet, all around me, the world seemed to be spinning out of control. Most of the people in my network were incredibly upset by the results of the presidential election. People everywhere were having problems wrapping their minds around the idea of Donald Trump in the White House. We were all living in a constant state of self-denial.

I decided to make the best of the situation. I doubled down on my activities in the community. I was excited by the prospect of teaching at John Jay College. I wanted to spread the message about hope and the power of education. I say this to people all the time: education is power.

When I first walked into BMCC as a professor on that first day of class back in 2011, I felt euphoric. The average person may not comprehend just how powerful that feeling was for a man who had once been homeless. One day I was sleeping in the subway, and the next I was conducting a class in front of a group of students. It was truly an amazing experience. Many of my trials and tribulations, my depression and struggle, through life came down to a matter of self-esteem. This opportunity to teach restored my sense of self-esteem and self-worth. I was convinced that education was the silver bullet for low self-esteem.

That's why when I got the call to teach at John Jay College, I jumped at the opportunity. I would even have the option to teach –human resource management. I would teach both grad and undergrad students. So, by the fall of 2017, I was now officially an adjunct professor at John Jay College.

As I approached the classroom for the first time, I started having flashbacks to 1978, to the first time I attended classes at John Jay College during my freshman year. I remembered my encounter with the police officer who nearly shot me. I was a student who was homeless at that time. Now, in the fall of 2017, I walked in through the door as a college professor. I looked at the security guard, and I smiled as I showed him my photo ID. The feeling was exhilarating.

My enthusiasm quickly spread to my students. During my very first semester as a professor, a student approached me to say that my class had inspired him to enroll in the doctoral program. I was overjoyed and stunned. This also made me a little bit nervous. I had not yet even completed my own Ph.D., but here I was inspiring students to pursue theirs. Wouldn't it be strange if they completed their degree before I did? I'm not sure my ego could handle that! So, in some ways, these students motivated me to get busy.

I was witnessing firsthand the magic of education and its power. I began to spread the word to not just college students but to anyone who would listen. On the one hand, I was carrying the message of hope. On the other hand, maybe my motives were selfish. As I talked to people about the magic of education and the beauty of pursuing your dreams, I was motivating myself to keep going.

I once again reached out to the group homes and nonprofit organizations in my community. I needed to get out and talk to people. Maybe it was a way to keep my spirits up. So, I would go to any group home, anywhere in the five boroughs. One of the group homes that I visited was in Washington Heights.

It was a program for teenage girls who were pregnant. Some of the girls were as young as fourteen years old, and most were not older than seventeen. The first group of six girls included four who were Puerto Rican, and two were black. The group home invited me to speak to this group at least once a week.

I must say that was one of the most interesting experiences I had interacting with a group of young people. However, my message was pretty much the same. I combined motivational principles with a message about education. I often took time to reminisce about my journey.

I often described the nights sleeping in the subways and the deep depression that consumed my life at that time. I began to see results not just from the people in the group homes, but also from many of the young people in school and outside the school.

Now, I was more motivated to complete my doctoral degree than ever before. My studies at Walden University were going very well. My first-year grade point average was 3.9. I was going into my second year of the program, and there was still much work to be done.

I had already started assembling my dissertation committee. I had met Dr. Jesse Lee, who was a business executive and a former police sergeant who also happened to be African-American. I hoped that he would agree to be the chairman of my committee.

Fortunately, Walden University gave me credit for some of the classes I had taken at the New School. However, I still had to repeat about ten classes. I doubled down and was able to complete those classes after a year and a half. Then, I could finally focus on my dissertation.

I was well aware that the dissertation process could take up to three years, However, I was very excited about the opportunity to move forward. I did a great deal of research about developing qualitative methods for a case study. I decided to focus on a study that examined the experiences of low-income young black men who were seeking employment in the current labor markets.

I had started on this subject during my final year in the Master's program at John Jay College. I had actually designed the framework for my study from my thesis. This study would allow me to not only use my thirty years of experience in the employment business but to design a study that would provide important insights regarding the experiences of unemployed, young, Black men. However, as with any study, I had to answer the first question. Which is- Who cares?

I was surprised to learn that not many people were interested in the problems of young, unemployed black men. I convinced myself that the subject was important, and I would dedicate my research project to that topic. I would need to find a nonprofit to use as a case study. I remembered what I learned from reading my books many years ago. I remembered the lessons about the opportunity. It oftentimes comes disguised as misfortune or disappointment. So, I knew that I should be on the alert. And, it actually did happen that way. Because of someone's misfortune, I met someone who would provide a pathway for me to complete my dissertation journey a year later.

THE EDUCATION ADVOCATE

At the start of 2018, the mood of the country shifted again. It was becoming more and more difficult to avoid conversations about the Trump administration, particularly during my classes at John Jay. In some ways, the classroom was a good outlet for me as well as the students to express our views. However, out of an abundance of caution, I decided to avoid political discussions. The political climate was hot and I could feel the tension in my classroom.

We now find more and more stories in the media about mass shootings. We hear about the tragedies happening at Marjory Douglas High School, and Santa Fe High School. People are feeling divided. We hear stories about the rise in racial tensions all over the country. It was sad to see Bill Cosby go to prison. However, no one should be above the law if they have done the wrong thing. Yet, it was painful. So many years ago, I would sit with my girls, and watch Cosby on television, and we would laugh, and enjoy the show. Now, I feel only sadness when I see his name.

I was now teaching as a full-time adjunct professor at John Jay College. My course schedule included five classes. My classes were often full, up to twenty-two students. So, most semesters I would teach up to a hundred students. I found more and more students reaching out to me about the doctoral program. Some students were already considering doctoral studies. Yet, there were quite a few who were not, until they joined my class. They would actually tell me that the idea to enroll in the doctoral program started once they joined my class.

One such student was Wally. I identified with Wally because he was a bit older than some in the class and a student of color. Wally also worked in the employment and staffing services. He later became interested in pursuing a doctorate in human resource management. One day he asked if we could get coffee and discuss the dissertation process.

When we met, he said, "I just submitted my application to the doctoral program, and I was really hoping that you could give me some advice so I can figure out why I got myself into this mess." We both laughed. I nodded my head. I understood that feeling. It's a feeling of mixed emotions, containing both the excitement of starting a new journey and the anxiety of anticipating challenges ahead.

I told him, "You will soon be very happy that you started this journey. You would have always questioned yourself if you hadn't. I know you're probably thinking about the fact that you're fifty-three years old and that this process takes four years. My only reply to you is if it takes four years or more, so what? By the grace of God, you're going to be fifty-seven anyway, so why not have a Ph.D.?"

That response got his attention. He lifted his head. He smiled. He looked directly into my eyes and nodded. I reassured him that I would be as supportive as I could be. I suggested that if he kept positive people around him, he would be successful on his journey.

As the year progressed, my students came to me one by one and expressed their desire to enter doctoral studies. I realized that I had become my former professor, Dr. Diih, who had wanted every student in his class to enroll in the doctoral program. Like him, I had become an education advocate.

My teaching style was somewhat pragmatic. I combined a few different methods. I would engage the students in the course work, and yet, blend my personal experiences. I would also blend the lessons with the events happening in real-time. For some reason, this worked. The entire class would participate in the discussion. In no time, the two-hour class was over. I always tried to hear from each student. I believe that every student should have a voice.

Sometimes I would encourage students to think about doctoral studies. However, I wasn't forceful about the idea. I just wanted to make students think about their potential. I especially wanted to encourage students of color. One student, Sarah, showed interest in enrolling in the doctoral program, and I didn't need to exaggerate when I told her that she had everything that was required to be a good doctoral student.

As I've said, I truly believed that education was a remedy for low self-esteem. It is not only empowering to the human soul, it has the power to remove self-doubt. It is also inviting because it is never too late in life to learn something new. I believed education provided hope. I was convinced that nothing could lift a person's spirit higher than walking across the stage at graduation time and accepting their degree from the president of the school. I also recognized that my motives were personal—by emphasizing this message of hope to my students, I maintained my commitment to the journey.

By the end of 2018, nearly half a dozen students had informed me that as a result of taking my class they were enrolling in the doctoral program. I was very excited about all of them. I had complete confidence that they would manage the journey. However, I was becoming more concerned about my progress.

I was still writing my dissertation and I had no guarantee that I would successfully defend it. I was also starting to get push-back from some faculty. I was starting to have flashbacks to the New School. This time was different, I really believed in my work. And, once again, I found myself in a place where failure was not an option. So, I went out into the community to talk with young people about entering the job market. It seemed that they lived in a world of "permanent recession". I would expand my network as well. I could achieve two goals at the same time.

I selected several nonprofit agencies that I had worked with years prior. One was the Doe Fund, an organization that assists homeless and formerly incarcerated individuals, who tend to come from underserved communities. The Doe Fund's main program was a workforce training program called *Ready, Willing & Able*, located on Porter Avenue in Brooklyn.

I collaborated with the Doe staff to develop workshops and seminars to help these individuals prepare for a changing job market. I provided information to participants to help with their transition process.

I conducted motivational workshops on-site and then I invited individuals to my office for mock interviews. My objective was to do everything possible to prepare each individual for entering the job market.

As I developed these workshops, I remembered the techniques that had helped me when I was getting off the streets. I often shared my experiences as a homeless man seeking employment. I often noticed how I captured the attention of the men once I spoke about my life as a homeless man. I then modified the framework of the Five C's that I learned from Dr. Dick Barnett. I described the concepts in a way that could benefit these young men.

For instance, I discussed the importance of being clear about your objectives, being consistent with your strategies, and committing to the pursuit of them. Always, I emphasized the importance of utilizing control. Many of these young men made progress as they prepared to enter the job market. Once again, I found examples of how education was magic. I also found examples of how opportunity comes disguised.

I was involved with several nonprofit organizations, including the Doe Fund. My involvement with that organization provided another benefit. As I mentioned before, on October 1, 2018, my older brother Richard was released from prison after nearly thirty-eight years of being incarcerated. I could tell during our last prison visits that he was concerned about how he would survive outside the prison.

A whole new world was waiting for him. I saw that he was really concerned about adjusting to this new world. I did my best to offer him some advice to address some of the questions that were nagging at him the most. Specifically, I told him about the Doe Fund.

If my brother Richard entered the Doe program, he would be provided all of the essentials that he needed. The program supplied a men's shelter to addresses housing needs and offered work options, such as helping in the kitchen as a cook. Some of the men were on the "street detail". Mostly, cleaning the streets and sidewalks.

They call it 'pushing the broom". The program was for nine months. Finally, Richard would be eligible to apply for public assistance and housing placement to help with adjusting to the long-term process of living on his own.

Some family members questioned if Richard's going into a men's shelter was a good idea. Most family members did not expect to see him for many years, and even he was not sure when he would be released from prison. It was a stroke of good fortune that his final parole hearing went well. On the eve of that hearing, I had traveled to the penitentiary to meet Richard to discuss his hearing strategy. My younger brother Nathaniel joined me.

My brother Richard had prepared all his paperwork and looked like a modern-day version of a jailhouse lawyer. He was prepared to go to his parole hearing and re-argue his case that he didn't do the crime he had been convicted of. Nathanial and I listened carefully to Richard, and when we looked at each other I could see that we were both thinking the same thing. We knew that it was too late to defend his innocence. We were thinking, "You have already served a twenty-five-to-life sentence".

However, we allowed our older brother to finish his argument. Then we advised him to take a different approach. We strongly recommended that he not even bring up the circumstances of the case.

I took a page from *The Shawshank Redemption.* I shared with Richard a quote from what Freeman's character says to his parole board: "I do deeply regret what happened to the person who lost his life and to his family, and the choices that I've made. I was a young, foolish man. If I had a chance to go back, I would warn myself, I would talk to that young man and tell him that he was going in the wrong direction, I would tell him there was no quick and easy way in life, and that in the end, we end up paying for everything. However, I cannot do that now, because that young man is long gone and all that is left is this old man sitting in front of you. I don't know how many more years I have left on this earth, but I can only hope that God will let me do something productive and meaningful with the remaining days of my life. And I hope that this board will allow me the opportunity to meet and reconnect with my family." I was looking at Nat, as I recommended these words to Richard. Nat agreed with his eyes.

Nat and I strongly recommended that Richard maintain that approach, and we drilled the words into his head. We repeated it again. As I spoke to Richard, his eyes fixed on me and he did not blink. At the end of our meeting, we gave him a big hug. Then we walked out of the visiting room.

I looked at Nat and we both shook our heads. We had our doubts. We were not at all sure that Richard would follow our advice. He was our oldest brother and he was the most stubborn of all the family members. But, we had given it our best shot.

Then, I got the news. When Richard wrote me a letter telling me that he been granted release from prison, I thanked God Almighty. I realized that Richard did not try to re-argue his case. He took a different approach, he followed our advice. I immediately started planning how to help him get ready for his release. This was a big deal. After thirty-eight years, the prodigal son was returning home. I knew he needed a place to live and he needed a place with structure. I did not agree that he should just move into a room in someone's house. It was not a good idea for a man who had spent nearly forty years in prison to walk out the door of the penitentiary and wake up the next day on someone's couch. No, he needed a program.

I believed the Doe Fund would be a good fit. They provided housing, food, and clothing for over four hundred men. Richard would not have to worry about these essentials for the next year. This was another lesson about the "sly disguise of opportunity," The Doe Fund provided a completely unexpected benefit to a family member. As far as my research study. That project developed because of a chance meeting at a hospital after I arrived with a stricken Dick Barnett. I met a man named Carlo in the waiting area. He was the manager of a nonprofit organization in Harlem that provided the framework to complete my dissertation study. During my journey back to Harlem, I would also make another discovery that would finally answer a question that has haunted me for fifty years. I would learn the identity of my real father.

CHAPTER 9

"'If we are related,' said the immortal Emerson, 'we shall meet.' In closing, may I borrow his thought, and say, 'If we are related, we have, through these pages, met."

Napoleon Hill

RENDEZVOUS WITH REALITY

By the end of 2018, I had been teaching at John Jay College for two years. At least four of my students had informed me that they had enrolled in the doctoral program. They all mentioned that one of the motivations for starting their doctoral studies was being a student in my class. They told me that they felt inspired. I did feel a bit of a boost to my ego. I even noticed that I did not share my experiences of being a homeless man anymore. It was difficult to determine if I stopped sharing my experiences because of some sense of shame. Yet, I was the first to say that it is critical to remember the past. Now, it seemed that I wanted to forget my humble beginnings. I spoke about these feelings with my support group.

I decided that I would continue to share these experiences, even with my students when it was helpful. As the year progressed, we were hearing more and more about students who were struggling financially. More students were unemployed, and many were homeless. We had conversations about the Trump administration, and what they called "a lack of leadership" It did feel like there was a real disconnect from the people who were struggling to survive. So, I sometimes shared my past experiences and even felt proud that I had come such a long way from my days as a homeless man.

I also struggled with another nagging question from my past. It was a question about my father. It was always there in the back of my mind. I would sometimes talk about it with my daughter Maxine. She decided to give me a birthday gift. So, a package arrived from a place called Ancestry.com. I sent back a saliva sample. I expected to learn more about my mother's family from the test. To my shock, I received an email from someone who claimed to know my real father.

I soon arranged a lunch with Dr. Eric Jarvis. He was a very interesting person. Polite, and professional in every way. We talked for a bit and enjoyed some lunch. Then he placed a group of photos on the table. There were three men dressed in their military uniforms. He said, "These three men are my uncles, and one of these men is your father" I was completed stunned.

I did not believe what he told me, despite the DNA evidence. He said, "It is likely, my Uncle Johnny, the man on the left". I looked at the photo and felt a chill down my back. I was thinking to myself "Is this the face that I have been searching some fifty years to find?" That man was John Henry Jarvis. It was just too good to be true. However, there was one person who would know. My Aunt Dolly, age 91, now living in Maryland.

My Aunt Dolly is our family matriarch and our treasure, and she is the only person who knows the whole history of our family. Whatever she says might as well be written in stone. I had sent her an email with a picture of the man named John Henry Jarvis attached, and she confirmed for me that he was in fact, my father. I felt a rush through my body. It was the most incredible feeling. For the first time in my life, I felt a sense of wholeness.

Aunt Dolly said, "Oh yes, I recognize John Jarvis. I remember him quite well. We talked often. He was the kind of man that stood out, very refined and very dignified. He was very proud of his military service."

I was bursting with anxiety and rushed to ask the most important question. "Can you tell me how he met my mother? Did they have a relationship?"

Aunt Dolly replied, "They sure did know each other, and it was pretty clear there was some type of relationship." I felt a delicious chill go down my spine.

She continued, "In fact, I do remember that my brother, Lester Lewis, who as you know was your mother's first husband, got into a fight with John Henry Jarvis." Wow! Did I need to hear more? Why are two men fighting? That is easy to answer. They are fighting over a woman. I was completely blown away, and at the same time excited.

I now had the answer to the question that had haunted me for years. I could finally put the name and the face together. I could look at a picture of my father. To my joy, he was not a man like Frank Williams. Jarvis was a very sharp, handsome man. I thought he looked like the actor Billy D. Williams. He was a World War II veteran. To my amazement, I learned that he had attended John Jay College of

Criminal Justice and became an attorney-at-law. I think that's pretty fascinating considering that now I am a professor at John Jay College.

I felt deep down inside that my mother could pick a winner every once in a while. I hope the two of them are looking from heaven now and are proud of what I've done, not only to restore my own life and clean myself up but to find true direction in my life and help others find a better path in life.

The Jarvis family is a family to be proud of. I was able to connect with several members of the family. In some cases, I even connected with other Jarvis family members who had never met. I found my cousin Sharon Jarvis. We met again with Eric, Maxine, and my grandkids, and had a wonderful lunch. I soon discovered that I have a nephew named Malik, who is the son of my brother Johnnie.

I learned about my great-grandmother Jennie Cailey, who was born on the Isle of Man in the United Kingdom. It was also funny to learn that my great-grandmother was a white woman. I learned that nearly all of my aunts and uncles served in the military during World War II. I hope to one day meet more family members from the Jarvis clan. My dream is to travel to the U.K., where I can find more of my family, and sit down and share a Guinness with folks related to Ms. Jennie Cailey.

However, back in New York, I planned another family gathering. My brother Richard was finally home, and ready to meet his family. We planned a family reunion for the start of 2019. Over the years, I had been able to stay connected to my siblings. Since I had organized the very first reunion in 1972, I made a point to attend every subsequent reunion no matter what, even when I was broke. I once attended a family reunion after losing all my money the night before at the racetrack. I spent that night at Barbara's house and borrowed some money from her the next morning when I left. I always believed that family was everything.

However, I was excited. I knew that this reunion would be very different because for the first time my oldest brother Richard would be in attendance. My brothers and sisters and all their families, including my daughter Maxine and my grandkids, met at Clyde Frazier's Wine and Dine in Manhattan. There, Richard saw family members he hadn't seen in over twenty years.

He met nieces and nephews who were born while he was in prison. The only person missing was my brother Gregory, who was living down in Florida.

I had scouted out the area the day before to make sure the restaurant could accommodate our large group. While out, I started to reminisce. My search for my scattered family began at the age of twelve and continued for five decades. I had struggled with deep depression for so many years when my family was taken away because I knew I had a right to be with my family regardless of the circumstances. A family gathering provided a feeling of "wholeness."

My search began by hounding social workers for answers, and then a chance meeting with my sister Barbara on the street. It took quite a bit of time to find all of my siblings. However, we were ultimately reunited and able to build a foundation. We got to know each other again. We helped each other out during difficult times. We had finally reached the point where we were a family not only from our genetics, but we had grown to love each other again.

I'm glad to say that my fifty-year obsession to find my family was worth the effort. In my heart, I knew that my family was the most important thing in the world, so I committed to always keep the connection to each family

For some years, my sister Susan had been working at Bailey Seton Hospital in Staten Island. Her daughter Tamara would later live with her godparents Irene and Pat. Tamara made us all so proud. She graduated with a master's degree and went on to become a public school teacher.

My sister Ruth joined the military. Later, when she retired, she dedicated her life to the church. Today she and her family live in Virginia, and they still join us for our reunions in New York.

My brother Nathaniel went on to achieve his dream of becoming a social worker and earned a doctoral degree in education. He now operates his own nonprofit agency that provides mental health services to disadvantaged groups.

My brother Juan decided on a career in the airlines. He has traveled around the world a dozen times with United Airlines and is now preparing to retire. He was another one of the family members who dedicated himself to keeping that bond with the family and doing everything possible to keep us together. He was a great help to our brother Richard during his transition back into the real world.

My brother Gerald had been adopted by a wonderful family at the age of three and spent most of his life living in Rochester. I sometimes communicated with his adoptive mother Carol on Facebook. She seemed like a really sweet lady. Gerald has worked in healthcare and recently decided to enroll at an online university. He did experience his own battles with depression and anxiety and made the effort to get back on the road to recovery. I am very proud of Gerald and all the progress he made against the odds.

My youngest brother Gregory surprised all of us by becoming a police officer. The circle of life had run its course. It's quite a surprise to have a little brother who was a police officer when you also have an older brother who was once in prison for murder. I am so proud of my photographs of Gregory in his uniform and with his K-9 dog. I knew he had made our mother quite proud. Gregory, his ex-wife Terra Lynn, and their son Garik had lived in Connecticut. Unfortunately, Greg went through a period of depression and anxiety. He moved to Florida and their marriage ended.

At the time of that reunion, I was enjoying my time teaching at John Jay College of Criminal Justice and I was still working with nonprofit organizations in my community. My own past experiences made me an asset to these organizations because sharing my own experiences as someone who was once unemployed and homeless was an effective way to connect with program participants. However, I was troubled by the fact that I could help strangers who were in need, and yet I could not help members of my own family who were facing real challenges. I found this quite puzzling.

Almost a year after my brother Richard came home from prison, he was still unemployed. I noticed that he struggled to adjust to this very different job market. Happily, in his time out he re-connected with a lady that he had known years prior. Her name was Susan, and they would later get married.

Richard was fortunate to find such a wonderful person. However, his unemployment situation still presented some real challenges. Yet, he was determined to keep the faith. Even during the pandemic, he managed to stay on the right track.

But there were other problems for me on the horizon. For instance, my staffing agency began a massive restructuring. Since the merger of our two companies, my future with the organization was really in doubt again. I was given notice my employment could end as of the second quarter of the year. I was being told that I would likely be out of a job in a few months.

I had known that business was not good, and yet I was still a bit surprised when the final decision. However, it was clear that the COVID-19 pandemic had a significant impact on that decision. The upside to my situation was that once again I was working with a company that had chosen not to put a contract in place. I did not have a non-compete to stop me from starting a new business.

The downside was the uncertainty of the pandemic. I was not sure if it was the best time to start my own company again. I was entering my fourth year in the doctoral program and was progressing with my dissertation, so I did not want to add too much to my plate. However, I was willing and able to start a new company if necessary. I could get it up and running while writing my dissertation. The future seemed challenging and unstable but filled with possibilities.

RESTORATION TIME

We had a really great re-union the past year. It was now 2019, and I was somehow still working with the Melville staffing agency. I was also teaching full-time at John Jay College of Criminal Justice. We had no idea that a pandemic was on the horizon. I was now considering a plan to start a publishing company. I was looking at all options as the year progresses. I also talked with some family members about another reunion, this time we wanted to include the entire family.

The New York Times reported that Donald Trump lost 1.7 billion dollars on his business deals. That seemed odd since he was the guy who wrote "The Art of the Deal". Then, we learned that a guy named Jeffery Epstein was found dead in his jail cell, a suicide. There were more stories about mass shootings. Next, a story that R. Kelly had been arrested. He was another guy fighting his demons. Finally, the news about the impeachment trial of Donald Trump.

As we arranged for the next family reunion, we knew that one person would be missing. My brother Gregory, the ex-police officer who moved to Florida. I often wondered if I could find him. Then, I got a phone call from my brother Nat that pretty much turned my day of sunshine into darkness again. It was one of the most depressing calls I could imagine. The call concerned my brother Gregory. Things had gone from bad to worse. Since he had gone through a divorce and had moved to Florida, he was not able to find employment. He had stopped taking his medication. He was struggling with a deep depression.

Gregory was the brother that I was most proud of. I always told new acquaintances about Gregory because he was a police officer. What I did not fully understand was just how challenging and difficult the job of a police officer was. I didn't know that the stress and depression of the job had taken a toll on my younger brother. Greg was unemployed and living day-to-day as a homeless man on the streets of Florida. Later we would learn that he was suffering from post-traumatic stress disorder and severe depression.

I was deeply saddened when I heard the news. Once again, that feeling of powerlessness came over me. I felt that previously I had failed when I tried to help my family members.

I had tried to help my nephews, cousins, and other family members. I could talk until I was blue in the face. Not much success. Oddly, I could motivate strangers but not family.

However, I knew that something needed to be done quickly, and so I made some phone calls. I contacted Greg's ex-wife Terri Lynn, my brother Nathaniel who was a social worker, and my brother Juan who worked for an airline. We decided to travel to Florida to find Gregory and intervene.

I was hopeful because my brother Nathaniel had many years of experience as a social worker and his ex-wife Terri Lynn had remained in touch with Gregory. Yet, I felt less confident about what I could do to reach him. I had only talked to my brother Gregory twice in the last twenty years. But, after talking with his wife and my brothers, we set the date and time for the trip. We discussed our plan and we said our prayers. We all wanted the same thing: to help Gregory and to see him get better. It was unfair that he had spent his whole life in law enforcement and was now living on the street like a destitute person. We felt that more had to be done for him.

Then, our plans fell apart. One by one, everyone canceled their plans to make the trip. First, Terri Lynn informed me that she could not make it due to a scheduling conflict that had come up at the last minute. Then, Juan mentioned that he would not be able to make the trip due to work obligations. Finally, Nathaniel canceled also because of last-minute obligations. My first thought was to simply reschedule the flight. The others said that they were willing to try again in a few weeks.

However, I started feeling that I needed to take the trip anyway. I cannot say for sure what caused this feeling within me. Something was pulling me to Florida. It was as if my mother was talking to me and was telling me, "Now is the time to see about your brother". I struggled with these emotions, almost wanted to say to my mother, "But I am not my brother's keeper."

Then, my feelings of guilt returned, and I knew I had to make that trip even if I had to go it alone. It was the least I could do for my mother. It was as if she was telling me, Go anyway, you will not be alone.

I was still struggling with a lot of mixed emotions as I paid for my airline ticket and booked my room. I was anxious about what I would say to Greg if I even found him. I wondered if he would recognize me. These questions nagged at me. When I spoke to Terri Lynn on the phone, she reassured me that Greg could be found at the same place every day. She said he was always in front of the barbershop next to the Dunkin' Donuts in Jacksonville. With that bit of information, I boarded a plane to Florida in search of a homeless man who had been on the streets for some time now.

I am not sure that Terri Lynn understood how flighty life is for homeless people. Quite easily, your plans can change. I couldn't help but think about how easily I could miss Greg. I could take that trip to Jacksonville, and that same morning Gregory might hitch a ride to Fort Lauderdale to earn a few dollars cleaning out a warehouse.

Yet, I felt that force pushing me to go, even encouraging me to go. So, I found myself at the airport with my suitcase, waiting for the plane to Jacksonville.

When I arrived at the hotel, I checked myself in and began unpacking my things. I had brought enough to read and to keep busy for the next two days. I was preparing for the possibility of not seeing my brother at all. Yet, I thought about all the books I read about positive thinking, I remembered the quote, "If you pray for rain, bring an umbrella". Yet, I decided not to get too comfortable in my room. Instead, I put on slacks and comfortable shoes. I called an Uber to take me to the location where I was told my brother could be found: near the Dunkin' Donuts on Atlantic Avenue.

This location was only a twenty-minute drive from the hotel. The driver of the car was very polite and seemed concerned about reports of shootings in the area. He mentioned how dangerous Jacksonville was for black men. He was a white guy, and I think he was trying to tell me to be careful in the area where I was heading.

I was preoccupied with thinking about how to find my little brother who was suffering from depression. I understood that a few social workers had come to talk to him without any success. They offered help in getting him off the street. He did not trust social workers. His ex-wife had also made several visits to see him.

She told me that at one point he did not remember the name of his former employer. All of this ran through my mind as the Uber turned onto the highway.

When I arrived, I immediately noticed that there was no barbershop near Dunkin' Donuts. I checked the area very carefully but saw no one there. I began searching the surrounding blocks for a barbershop without any success. I walked for blocks and was quickly becoming discouraged.

I then crossed over the highway and I went into a small convenience store. I also checked the gas station. No luck. I looked and looked but I could not find my little brother. Now, I was becoming frustrated and feeling a little bit dumb, thinking about the money I had spent on the plane ticket and the hotel. I thought I'll just go back to the hotel and fly home tonight. Then, a voice in my head told me to check back across the street. There was a ladies' beauty salon there. It felt odd to check a ladies' beauty salon, but the voice in my head was clear. Go.

The beauty salon was closed, but a black man was sitting on the ground with his back against the wall, staring at the sky. He was young and muscular. I searched his face very hard to see if I recognized any of his features. Our eyes met and the man spoke. He said, "Mike? Is that you?"

He really seemed to be saying, "Mike? You came here for me?"

I couldn't react. I froze. In a second, a little bit of electricity ran through my body. Then Greg stood up, all six-feet-two-inches and two hundred and twenty-five pounds of him. I had found my baby brother! Thank you, Jesus.

I said, "Man, I was worried I couldn't find you! I was looking here and there and thought I had the wrong place. How are you doing?" He smiled at me. It was that same smile like that picture I had taken when he was just a baby.

I was at a loss for words and was saying anything that popped into my head. In my nervousness, I suggested that we get some lunch. He thought for a moment. He smiled again. He liked the word "lunch." So, he said, "I can certainly eat something right now."

I asked if he knew a place to eat nearby. He suggested Denny's one block over. I thought "great" Let's go to Denny's. Despite something negative I once read, it sounded great. We started walking towards Denny's. He hesitated, then asked, "Mike, can I order a sirloin steak?"

I smiled and said, "That's a great idea. I'll order one too."

We walked into Denny's, and we were seated pretty quickly. As we talked over lunch, I saw signs of the difficulties of his plight. He struggled to talk. He mentioned that he been waiting for months for a phone call from a former employer. I told him it was unlikely that he would ever get a call from his former boss and besides, he needed to get a phone first. He told me that he had had a phone but had sold it to get some food. This I understood.

I talked a lot but was not really sure what to say. The Denny's waitress, a white lady in her late forties, was very polite. She seemed to know Greg and seemed happy that I was bringing him there for lunch. I had brought some family photos with me to share with Greg.

I decided to show him the photograph of our mother that I had taken on her fortieth birthday, the last photo was ever taken of her, taken when we had no idea that we would lose her four months later. I also showed him a picture that I had taken of him as a little baby boy in his crib. He had that amazing smile on his face. It had given me a reason to use my new camera.

Our eyes met across the lunch table, and I started to talk about my own experience as a homeless person. I talked about my life for a while. I talked about my many trips to the racetrack with my empty suitcase. Then, I talked about why I had made the journey to find him. However, I decided not to question him about his own experiences living on the streets.

At first, sharing my experiences did not seem to connect with him at all. I felt like I was talking in a different language. I talked about my problem with gambling and going to casinos and losing a lot of money, but I could tell by his eyes he was not able to follow.

Yet, I knew from my years of talking to young men and women on the streets that reaching someone who has experienced homelessness and depression is like trying to find a station on a radio.

I just had to play with the knob until I turned to the right station. Sometimes, I just had to turn the knob just a hair to the left, and then I find the station. So, I decided to keep talking until I said something that got his attention.

I began to talk to Gregory about how I got off the streets. I told him about having that cup of coffee with a stranger. This was what I called "Restoration Time" So, I described to him how I got a job as a nighttime security guard after being on the street for almost three years. I told him how often, when I went home to my room, I couldn't sleep in my bed. The bed was too clean and the room was too quiet. I told him about how I used to get up from my bed each night at 3 a.m. and sleep on the trains.

As I told him how I needed the shaking and the noise of the train to put me to sleep, I noticed that he was really listening now. We had tuned into the right radio station. So, I started to tell him that I had broken my cycle of homelessness the same way someone might break an addiction to a drug. I did my best to explain that homelessness is a condition. A type of emotional condition. To break the cycle almost requires a kind of detox approach. In other words, it is all about changing behavior.

I talked for a few more minutes and then I called the waitress over for the check. As we got ready to leave, I told Gregory that despite his setbacks, I was proud of him. Then my Uber arrived and it was time to say goodbye. I said a prayer for my brother before I left. I believe our mother was looking over us from above, and she wanted her son to do better. I looked at the picture of him as a police officer in his uniform. I wanted him to know that I still believed in him. I believed our mother was proud of him, too. I also had some hope that somehow, his situation could get better.

I promised Greg that I would keep in touch and I gave him some pocket money. I also wrote my phone number on a piece of paper and told him to call me collect anytime.

As I flew home, I knew I had done my best to help my little brother. However, midflight, the feeling of helplessness came over me again. I wondered if Greg would even remember that I was there that afternoon. It seemed that his memory had really deteriorated. Would he even remember my words?

Two weeks later, I got a call from his ex-wife Terri Lynn. She told me that Gregory had gotten in touch with a social worker. He was now willing to provide information to them that he had simply refused to provide in the past, including personal information like his social security number. He no longer wanted to be the invisible man. Greg had decided to get off the street.

A few weeks later, near the end of December, one of the social workers informed me that Gregory was living in a hotel. In a few weeks, the COVID-19 pandemic would begin to wreak havoc everywhere, including Florida. By February 2020, Gregory had moved into a one-bedroom apartment. I sent him a few items for his new place.

I was happy that he was off the street before the COVID-19 pandemic really began the spread. I was so grateful that I had listened to the voice in my head and went to Florida to find my brother. Even today, I am so proud of his service in law enforcement. I am so proud of the fact that he was a police officer for so many years. I was also thankful to know that I had found the last missing member of my family. I especially was grateful that I had been actually able to help not only a family member but the youngest member of my family, my baby brother. There was this old-school song. I could hear it playing in my head. By the group "War" called, Me and Baby Brother, me and baby brother, used to run together, Oh yeah, me and baby brother, used to run together.

When I put my head on the pillow that evening, I could hear my mother's voice quietly telling me, "Good work, my son, I wanted you to go look after my baby, and you did. I love you. You are still my favorite."

That night, I slept like a rock.

UNFINISHED BUSINESS

I will always remember 2020 for a lot of reasons, beginning with the COVID- 19 pandemic. Like some evil spirit, the virus seemed to come out of nowhere. The year started with much attention on the Trump Administration and the possibility of seeing a president impeached for the first time since President Bill Clinton. Then, I heard a report that Kobe Bryant was killed, along with his daughter. The news was extremely sad. Being the father of two girls, it was really beyond my ability to comprehend. Little did I know it was the beginning of a most tragic year. At the start of the year, my mind was consumed with problems in business and at school.

I was still teaching five classes at John Jay College of Criminal Justice and was happy to be one of the full-time faculty. It was a bit challenging holding two full-time jobs, and managing my doctoral studies. Yet, I enjoyed the challenge. It was another sign that my obsessive-compulsive behavior was working in my favor. I was still finding ways to put the enemy to work for me.

The experience of teaching at the college was becoming quite powerful. Some of my students were still telling me that they were inspired by my classes, and some had enrolled in the doctoral program. Again, I felt pressure as I was running into some difficulty with my own dissertation experience. Once again, I was having flashbacks from my experiences at the New School. Specifically, the process with my committee was endless and exhausting.

I have had experiences with professors who seemed to operate from a position of trying to frustrate their students as they try to achieve their goals. I don't understand this rationale and did not want to believe that a professor would ever get pleasure from frustrating a student who was trying to complete a degree. And yet, I had heard stories about students who even quit school after being frustrated by their professors. So, even though I was approaching the end of my dissertation project, the path forward was less clear.

The process of completing a dissertation can be more than just exhausting, it can turn into a form of torture. I was starting to feel some stress. However, I was fortunate to have a chair of my committee. Dr. Lee was from the school of positive thinking.

I wonder if he ever read Napoleon Hill. So, he tried to encourage me to continue with my dissertation.

Then, COVID-19 exploded everywhere.

Because of COVID-19, many students at Walden had to walk away from their doctoral studies. However, I was committed to finishing this eight-and-a-half-year journey. When I logged on for my class that week, I was the only student left in my group. Every other student had decided to drop out, and return for the Spring 2021 term. I decided not to quit. I decided to find a way to turn this situation around. Once again, I wanted to turn this liability into an asset. I always tell people that life is a game. I repeated to myself, "The game is not over until I win."

The lockdown began in March. My employer first transitioned me to work remotely. John Jay College moved all my classes to remote learning. My entire world shifted into a remote model I hated the idea of being home alone. I knew because of the pandemic that I would not have any visitors. I was having trouble meeting people before the pandemic. I was not even going out on any dates. I wanted to complete my degree before getting involved in a relationship.

I learned a lesson when I set up a lunch date with a woman I met at the Friday happy hour party a few years before. She was a lawyer, a black woman, and very attractive. As we were talking, I told that I had two full-time jobs, I was completing my doctoral degree. She politely told me that I do not time for a relationship and should not waste her time. She then walked out of the restaurant. I was really disappointed. That was my last date for a while. I later re-connected with Monique.

So, now comes the lockdown. I felt trapped inside my apartment, and for a moment I almost panicked. I knew that I have too much energy to be in lockdown.

It should not be surprising that an individual with an obsessive-compulsive personality would start to panic under the conditions of a lockdown. I also expected that my "triggers" would go off. So, I was also struggling with fear, which, historically, has motivated me to want to run. However, this time I couldn't escape to Atlantic City because it was closed. Yet, I noticed that online gambling was everywhere.

They even offer to give a person some money to get started. I was starting to feel some anger. That can also be a trigger. Then, I thought about my mom. I remembered that my mother used to say, "When life gives you lemons, make lemonade."

I decided to get busy. I had somehow managed to submit all my work, all of my research and my final two chapters, to my committee before the lockdown, but I still had to prepare for my dissertation defense. So, the lockdown provided me time to think about my defense day. I decided the quarantine would be an opportunity for me to test everything I've learned in life. I could test my theories about motivation and reinventing my life. I could test my theory of redirecting energy to achieve positive goals. In a lockdown, I would have an opportunity to focus my attention on two important tasks: completing my dissertation and writing my first book.

For many students, the dissertation defense is a make or break moment. I scheduled my defense for late July. I also decided not to tell anyone that I was scheduled to defend my dissertation.

The morning of my dissertation defense had arrived. I was a bit on edge. I did not sleep that well the night before. I still did not tell a soul about what I was up to. I did not want the attention on me. I had rehearsed my presentation over and over again like it was a role in a play. My notes were written out and taped all over the wall in my living room. My dissertation defense would consist of a conference call and a PowerPoint presentation.

I put on Pavarotti that morning to help me focus. Luciano Pavarotti was one of the greatest tenors of all time. I had started listening to him the year before and I had fallen in love with his voice. Something about his singing allowed me to be at peace. Then, as Pavarotti played, I took a nap. At noon, I called into the online conference, where the members of my committee waited. I felt like the star of a Broadway show.

The chair of my committee spoke first, Good afternoon Michael, I hope you are well, I will start to record this meeting, and you can start your presentation now. Then, for some reason, I could still hear Pavarotti singing in my ear as I presented each step of my research project.

I started with the introduction, the background of the case study, then my research problem, the research purpose, the research question, then the relevance of the project to the literature, then relevance to the theoretical framework, then the implications for social change, and then to my summary and conclusion. The words just seemed to flow out like music.

Standard protocol is that the committee calls the defendant later in the day with their verdict. I did not wait long. I quickly received the news that my dissertation was approved. I did it! I made it! Receiving that news was a moment of complete exhilaration and excitement. I was counting my blessings and feeling a deep appreciation for all the things that had happened to me in my life.

Just as quickly, my mind was flooded with thoughts of all the work that remained in front of me. I could hear the voice of Dr. Martin Luther King, Jr., telling me to keep marching on—that there was no turning back now. I remembered the books I had read while homeless and hiding out in the library. I remembered the principles of motivation that I'm guaranteed to succeed if I persist. Finally, I reminded myself about the Five C's.

My first reaction was to call my ninety-one-year-old Aunt Dolly in Maryland. She was absolutely thrilled for me and reminded me that it was my determination that made the difference.

Next, I called my former college professor Dr. Stanley Diih. His excitement was palpable. In the space of thirty seconds, he called me "Dr. Williams" four times. I reminded him of our first-class when he planted the seed in my mind of enrolling in the doctoral program

I had another reason to feel encouraged and hopeful. I had started to write a book about my life, and now I could complete the book. The book would be about my journey of redemption and a story of reconciliation. You have now read that book. As part of this experience, I also decided to start a new publishing company called Outerbridge Books, LLC. A publishing house where anyone and everyone could write their first book. I believe inside each person there is a story to be told and a book waiting to emerge.

In addition to my other ventures, I hope to connect with those people and help them bring that book to the surface. I hope that some of the people who read this book, will now contact me. I can help write your story.

To me, the universe is full of learning and full of stories, and there are no diplomas or graduation dates for the school of life. The world is a school where you continue to learn until your last day on this earth. And only once you've been dead and buried for three days then have you officially graduated.

I made a trip to visit Monique again in New Jersey. She lived ten minutes from Atlantic City. It was difficult to take that bus ride. But, I really wanted to see her, and I knew it was better not to rent a car. I accepted the fact that I was a terrible driver. So, I would take the 2-hour bus ride with the other people who were going to the casino. I would get off the bus before the stops at the casino. Strange, I was the only passenger to get off at the terminal.

Somehow, the relationship worked. Even my trust issues did not create any real problems. We were in a pandemic, so it was great to be able to get together when we could. So, we did.

In late October, I decided to arrange a small family reunion. It was warm for that time of the year, and we found a great spot for outdoor dining. I left my apartment early to take the train to meet everyone. I kept looking at my watch as I was walking toward the train station. I was planning to take a train to meet my daughter and grandkids, and then we would ride together to the reunion. I was running about an hour early to meet them, but as always, I had brought a book to read.

As I reached the train station at 23rd Street and Seventh Avenue, a young man approached me very timidly. He was wearing a mask to protect himself during the COVID-19 pandemic and I was wearing my mask as well. He spoke to me without removing his mask. His voice was so low, I could barely hear him.

He said, "Excuse me, sir, I don't mean the trouble you, but I haven't had a thing to eat in nearly two days. Can you help me get a cup of coffee?"

His voice, strangely familiar, sent a chill down my back. I still had a trained ear and I could tell the phonies from the real deal. This young man was the real deal. This young man, well, reminded me of someone. I felt like I had come face to face with my own ghost. At first, I was at a loss for words. I often just walk by the homeless without even a glance.

I looked over his shoulder saw an outdoor café with a couple of empty chairs and tables, and a waiter standing nearby. I decided the reunion could wait a while I stopped to have coffee with this young man. Who knows—this could end up being an interesting conversation.

So, I looked at the young man and asked, "Would you like to have a cup of coffee together?" The young man nodded politely.

As we began walking towards our seats, my mind was racing. I felt some very powerful emotions. I was not sure why. I had many conversations with young men in the past, I met many lost souls trying to find a path forward. But, there was something different about this young man. We took out seats and ordered some food and coffee. I started to speak. I am thinking that I should choose my words carefully, why? Because a life could change in these next few minutes. I looked this young man straight in his eyes. I told him that I was a college professor, and not long ago, I was sleeping in the subways.

Our eyes locked. I began to speak again. Once again, carefully selecting each word. Because in the back of my mind, I am thinking - he is really listening, and then, I realized that this could be a turning point.

This is what I called "restoration time" or what I now like to call "resurrection time".

Made in the USA
Middletown, DE
16 May 2021